This Gardening Business

There are no set rules for the way
a True Plantsman dresses.

Nigel Colborn

✦✧✦✧✦✧✦✧✦✧✦✧✦✧✦

This Gardening Business

✦✧✦✧✦✧✦✧✦✧✦✧✦✧✦

With illustrations by
Nick Wright

CASSELL

Cassell Publishers Limited
Artillery House, Artillery Row
London SW1P 1RT

Copyright © Nigel Colborn 1989
Illustrations Copyright © Cassell 1989

First published 1989

British Library Cataloguing in Publication Data

Colborn, Nigel
This gardening business.
1. Gardening — Humour
I. Title
635'.0207

ISBN 0 304 31642 3

Typeset by
Litho Link Limited, Welshpool, Powys, Wales

Printed in Great Britain by Mackays of Chatham Plc

For the twins

Matthew and Alexandra
Thomas and Susannah

Contents

Chapter 1

~~~~~~

Who Are the Real Experts?

~~~~~~

'What is a hardy perennial?'

(Kenneth Becket, *Growing Hardy Perennials,*
Croom Helm 1981)

Gardening expertise is one of today's biggest growth industries. Every week a new personality erupts from the media bounding with erudition and enthusiasm. An hour or two of study could put you into the limelight too. You don't have to have a garden – you don't even need a window-box as long as you have the ability to be *convincing.* Qualifications are not necessary – a university degree in horticulture would be a distinct disadvantage – for being a garden expert is not just a profession but a way of life.

As with sailing or hunting, it's all a matter of speaking the right language. This is much more important than actually being able to do anything very clever. Understanding the language of plantsmen is essential but not nearly as difficult as you might think. It is also important to find out how to develop those subtle little traits one has come to associate with the established experts. A thick regional accent used to be considered necessary for this, but in these days, when Old Etonians are taking classes in cockney so that they can further their political careers, the broad dialect doesn't cut quite such a dash. An alternative, favoured by some television experts, is to display a kind of hysterical rapture over every plant irrespective of whether it has any garden merit or not. The technique consists of drooling over specimens at Chelsea like a small boy given free rein in a chocolate shop. Somewhere in between these styles you will probably find your niche.

As with other vocations, there are several types of expert and you'll need to know which category is going to suit you best. Once decided, you will have to think about developing your approach. Everything must be right, from dress to language, but a true and deep knowledge of actual gardening, though it has its place, is not vital. Above all, you must develop the technique of using scientific names. *Do not let this requirement put you off – it's not as daunting as it sounds!* You don't need to memorise more than a handful of Latin mouthfuls and, anyway, learning the names of too many plants is pointless because the botanists are constantly re-classifying them. The main knack is to be able to reel off impressive-sounding words at the right time. You will soon discover that everyone is as confused as you are about which is the true scientific name anyway.

For the sake of creating some sort of order, the various categories of expert are described as follows.

The True Plantsman

The True Plantsman must be incredibly old. There is a rule that nobody in horticulture can really know his plants until he has been collecting for at least half a century. This makes the True Plantsman – let's call him a TP from now on – a pretty rare bird. In most professions, as members slide into old age their judgement becomes suspect, but the TP is more like a judge or politician, and is therefore not taken very seriously until he is well into his upper eighties.

There are no set rules for the way a TP dresses. Typically he might wear an ancient Panama hat and will often have a red spotted hanky in the breast pocket of his old tweed jacket. More eccentric TPs may turn up at flower shows with string tied round beneath their knees – presumably to prevent garden pests from crawling up their trouser legs and attacking their vitals. Some have even been known to wear gaiters.

There are women TPs of course, and their dress is similar but usually more masculine. Female TPs are not often seen in gaiters these days but the most famous one ever to have lived – Gertrude Jekyll (always reverently referred to as *Miss* Jekyll) – had a splendid pair of hobnail boots which were made immortal by the artist Sir William Nicholson.

TPs' habits are sometimes remarkable. They usually frequent the leading flower shows, serving as judges on the standing committees or just mingling with their kind. One way of getting into the Chelsea Flower Show on the Monday (the day the Queen goes) if you are not a member of the press or staging a display, is to submit a specimen for consideration by a Floral Committee. When a TP does this it will not be a new hybrid rose or dahlia, but will more likely consist of an extraordinarily odd item collected from the wild in some horribly inaccessible territory: a tree parsnip from the Falklands perhaps, or a giant groundsel from Mount Kenya. Most TPs are wonderful entertainers and will reminisce for hours about the good old days when one could employ three trustworthy gardeners for the price of a dram, with sixpence change.

The TP's garden will never be anything short of fascinating. It will always house a huge collection of special plants and, more often than not, will be well laid out and lovingly cared for. His house will be full of flowers too. Not well-executed arrangements *à la* Constance Spry, but odd specimens that have been broken off by the wind, or culled for closer observation. Most TPs are generous to a fault and will press you to accept seeds and cuttings from their treasures. A true plant lover is never mean with plant material for it is always in his nature to want to proliferate the species and varieties he loves.

In spite of his age, the TP will have a near-perfect memory. Frequently, this memory will prove the most reliable reference books to be wrong. Unlike the rest of us, for whom colour and scents become indistinct in the mists of time, the TP can recall, in every and precise detail, all the subtle tones, shapes and textures of a plant he may not have seen for 50 years. This makes him invaluable for identifying many of the botantical bygones that are creeping back into cultivation these days. More often than not his verdict will disagree with the name the nurseryman is using for the plant in question. However, like the Pope, the TP's word is 'The Truth' so all the grower has to do is change the name in his catalogue.

How to Become a True Plantsman

The chief ingredient is time. It's like the old story about the American tourist who asked the head gardener at one of the

Cambridge colleges how he managed to have such perfect lawns.

'Just cut 'em and roll 'em,' says the gardener.

'That all?' asks the incredulous visitor.

'Ah!' affirms the gardener.

'How long for?'

'About four hundred years.'

It takes nearly as long to become a TP. Actually, many of the most famous – great names like E. A. Bowles and William Robinson spring to mind – are dead and gone, so like becoming an immortal poet, you can't really get your act together until you've been buried for a few years. You will need to have written at least one good book and preferably two or three. It would be better if these were written while you are still alive but, judging by some of the garden literature about these days, much is written posthumously.

Travel is important too. Your average TP will have been all over the world and his garden will be populated with material collected on various expeditions. You will be treated to lengthy anecdotes about how the various treasures were snapped up.

'That is the only example of *Primula clotworthyana* in England,' he might say. 'Had to lower a native down on a sixty-foot rope for that when I went to Sikkim in '81.' (He won't specify the century and it would be rash to assume he meant 1981.) 'Had to lower 'im twice too. First time down the silly beggar forgot to take his trowel!'

If, like most of us, you are daunted by the prospect of having to wait so long to become a TP, don't despair. The next best thing is to become a **Budding Plantsman.** This is a kind of transitional stage and most garden experts fall into this category.

The Budding Plantsman

This is by far the largest category of garden expert. There are various stages of development. Age and experience are not necessarily as important as having met the right people or done the right things. Once someone is recognised as a BP he is regarded with an esteem which increases as he gets older.

A BP should have a deep and thorough knowledge of plants. Few do. Most make up for the deficiency in various ways. Specialisation is always useful and there is many a BP who will know and recognise every species, sub-species and variety of one genus, and very little about anything else. Here's an example:

How to collapse a Galanthophile

Imagine you are showing a galanthophile round your garden:
'That's a fine example of *Galanthus ikariae latifolius*' he'll remark, adding disconcertingly, 'if it really is.' He'll then turn up the flower of the poor little snowdrop and look thoughtfully at its private parts. (You knew it was a snowdrop didn't you? – of course you did. Anyway, even if you didn't you should have nodded sagely to yourself and kept mum.) 'Where did you get this from? Kostebom Dutch bulb specialists? Mm, thought so. They've sold loads this year under that name. Quite wrong of them. It's pretty common of course. Just an unnamed hybrid.'
'But I paid £4.50 for a single bulb,' you reply, horrified.
'Mm. You have to know what you're doing with snowdrops. Why've you got all those masses of ordinary *Galanthus nivalis* growing over there? They're not rare or anything.'
'I like them. They look lovely in February, you know, in drifts.'
'But why not have drifts of *Galanthus* 'Straffan' or 'Sam Arnott'? They're so much more special.'
'I like plain old common snowdrops!' Galanthophile stares with scandalised expression and adopts a second tack: 'Have you tried *Galanthus nivalis* sub-species *reginae-olgae?* or *G. corcyrensis?*' (Isn't it extraordinary that these people can talk in italics!)
'No.'
'Oh, you should. They flower in October.' The only fit reply to which is: 'Surely, they'd be completely lost amongst all those enormous Michaelmas daisies?' Partial collapse of Galanthophile.
If you know your plants, however, you could say: 'Mm. I prefer the autumn snowflake, you know, *Leucojum autumnale;* so much more refined, and less nasty foliage in the spring!' You could leave off here but a final *coup de grâce* would be to drop a name thus: 'I was very taken with them at Lady Viola Testerbed's. She has drifts of them in her scree at Meubles Hall. I'm sure Vi would let you have a few bulbs if I asked her on your behalf. In fact she'd

probably have swapped them for some of your snowdrops if she weren't custodian of the International Snowdrop Collection.'

The beauty of specialising is that you can display a deepish knowledge, albeit in a very narrow field, after a short spell of intense study. However, you won't be able to fool all horticulturists all of the time. To broaden your knowledge further, a little more work is required. This need not be too irksome, for it is always possible to develop at your chosen pace. Collecting plants that belong in your special subject will help you to get to know other BPs, and once you feel you are well on with your first plant family you can begin on another.

As in all aspects of the British way of life, with plants there is a rigid class structure. You will need to decide whether you are likely to be more comfortable with fuchsias and pelargoniums at one end of the scale or rhododendrons and camellias at the other. A guide to the social standing of plants is included in a later chapter.

Knowledge alone cannot turn a BP into a garden expert. The personality has to be right as well. Many BPs in the public domain can be seen to cut a special dash so that their image is unmistakable. Some use clothing for this, resorting to jackets without sleeves or developing monumental side whiskers. Certain television characters have been known to perform in the same pullover for several seasons, sleeping in it between recordings in order to help viewers feel less shabby themselves.

There are BPs who make it their business to know all the gossip and spread the news far more effectively than the pressmen. These can be heard in action at horticultural gatherings:

'You know Helen – not the one that ran off with Dickie, the one who got that gold medal at Harrogate for the *Fritillaria gussichae* (well, she would wouldn't she, knowing that dishy judge as well as she does) – well, anyway, guess what? She's only been caught pinching cuttings! And guess where?? At the Chelsea Physic Garden!!! Yes. Dropped her handbag on the way out. When the gardener handed it to her the catch flew open. Well, she could hardly close it. It was crammed full of greenery. Mind you, talking of gardeners, have you met hers? Ooer! talk about weird. Oh no, my gawd, she's perfectly safe from him, it's Cedric I'd be worried about. What they get up to in that greenhouse – no, Cedric, you

know, Helen's husband – went to Kathmandu. Alone . . .'
Overhearing a conversation like that will soon teach you to play
your cards close to your chest, unless, of course, you want
something broadcast.

Many BPs strive for recognition as gardening experts by
submitting specimens of their favourite plants to the Royal
Horticultural Society for an Award of Merit. This is a quaint
custom which has more to do with the personalities of the judges
than the plant's actual merit. After all, how can you tell how good
a given plant is by looking at a broken-off branch or two? What
happens is that you take your treasure to an RHS flower show at
Vincent Square. One of the so-called floral committees will then
pass it round a table and decide whether or not they like it.

An Award of Garden Merit is a different kettle of fish of course.
To win one of those your plant has to go through trials at the RHS
garden at Wisley, Surrey. More objective, but it only tells you how
good a plant is in the gentle climate of Southern England. If you
live north of King's Lynn, don't assume the winner of an AGM
will be any good for you.

If you are lucky enough to develop a really stunning new plant –
either by careful breeding or by a happy accidental cross in your
garden – this will be a first-class subject to submit to a floral
committee. Never expect any results until it has been submitted at
least twice. Remember, there will be at least one True Plantsman
on the committee reviewing your new cultivar and he may well
remember it as an introduction from the 1920s and be able to tell
you that you have misnamed it.

A BP's garden will usually be too small to house his growing
collection. At this early stage in his career as an expert the
numbers of different plants in his possession will be more
important to him than fancy landscaping. He will rationalise about
his muddly planting, saying things like: 'Plants make a garden, all
the rest is subordinate', or, 'Of course, I go in for totally
naturalistic planting.' Which means that however interesting a
collection it may be, it's still a mess.

Some BPs are upwardly mobile and will have a good many of
their prized rarities constantly growing in containers so that they
can keep moving house without having to do a mass of digging.
Unlike old cottagers, yuppies abhor growing things in old chimney
pots. Indeed, many of them spend their weekends ferreting about

old cottages in the hopes of persuading their occupants to sell their nicely planted chimney pots so that they can empty them out, cart them back to Peckham Rye and Fulham and put them on their restored chimney stacks.

The BP's constant *cri de coeur* is 'Oh for somewhere bigger where we can really develop a garden!' Some manage to do this by selling up in town and buying a decrepit manor house somewhere in the middle of the shires. In their naïvety, they think the price drop between their London villa and the romantic rural abode will enable them to invest the difference. But, before long, when the first January gale has blown off half the roof and mortar bees have regrouted the pointing with their own interesting pattern of holes, they realise that what had seemed a snip at a hundred thou is going to cost that much a year to keep in one piece.

At some stage in their plans an idea emerges of trying to finance the garden by starting an especially interesting plant nursery. They will buy a greenhouse or a couple of plastic tunnels and begin propagating. Not for them the bedding plants, rose trees and conifers. No, they'll be selling choice perennials, ancient hybrids, rare cottage garden gems, and boy, will they be charging for them! I mean like *real* money!

The handsome profits they expect to make in the nursery will provide useful funds to spend on the garden. By the time they are established and have been trading for a while they will have graduated to the next category of expert.

The Nurseryman

As BPs soon find out, it's nearly impossible profitably to run (I'm quite happy to split perennials but to carelessly split an infinitive – never!) both a fine garden and a commercial nursery at the same time. Established nurserymen are much better at telling other people how to run their gardens than they are at gardening themselves. There are a few notable exceptions, of course, but, by and large, gardens and nurseries don't go together.

At this point it should be stressed that a nursery has absolutely nothing in common with a garden centre. Garden centres are places where people who know next to nothing about plants flog what they think the public will want. They don't usually grow them on the premises but buy them in from various wholesalers. Garden centres are places to buy tools, outdoor furniture, gardening books, barbecue things and Christmas decorations. They are not suitable for serious plant purchasing.

Garden centres are usually on busy roads and are easily accessible. A plantsman's nursery, on the other hand, will be sited in a remote spot, difficult to find, and will usually be closed when you arrive. It may well be a small family firm, so arriving at lunchtime invariably results in a slightly forced smile on the face of the proprietor. There are certain rules that should be obeyed when visiting specialist nurseries. The greatest of these is *never* to call the place a garden centre or market garden. This causes deep offence because you must remember that the nurseryman, even if he is far too busy to have a real garden of his own, is almost certainly a Plantsman, and may well be an aristocrat to boot. It demeans him to suggest he is a garden centre for he grows his own stock and regards himself as an artist. Market gardeners produce things like lettuce for market and few would know the difference between *Paeonia mlokosewitschii* and *Eupatorium purpureum*.

Another golden rule for inexperienced nursery callers is *never* to start picking up plants until you are absolutely sure they are for sale. Many nurserymen will cunningly mingle their stock plants and other reserved items among their retail ware so that an unwary customer could get his head bitten off for muddling up, say, a range of unnamed Auriculas which are foundation stock and won't be on general sale for another three years.

Many customers will ask for something to put their purchases in. This is extremely inconsiderate and will naturally cause offence. There may well be a hundred used Dutch tomato trays, several dozen chip baskets and a welter of cardboard boxes all piled round the selling area. However, these are not available as the nurseryman will want to keep them for other uses. He probably doesn't yet know what he wants them for but he'll think of something one day. Meanwhile, they make a useful windbreak and *you can't have them*.

It's worthwhile making sure you have the right change. If you don't, the nurseryman will have to disappear to his house –

sometimes this may be several miles away – to raid his piggy bank for some coins.

Unlike most garden centres, a good nursery will always have someone on the premises who can tell you, in considerable detail, about the plants for sale. He (or she – I don't mean to be sexist – perhaps you should regard the 'he' as being common gender) will be happy to provide you with plenty of cultural advice as well. This doesn't mean throwing in his two penn'orth about what they're doing especially well at the English National Opera this year, but how best to grow your plants. Most of his advice is sound, but one must remember that he has an axe to grind and some of what he says may be coloured with commercial expediency. The following translations should help:

Viola 'Vita' is just right for your soil and luckily we have some to spare this week.
We have a surplus of 'Vita' because nobody else likes it.

It will take a season to settle in.
It probably won't survive but, by the time it dies, with any luck you'll have forgotten where you bought it.

We have them, but they are not ready to go yet.
They're way the hell down the other end of the nursery and I'm not sure I can find them.

We found they didn't sell very well.
We never mastered the art of growing them.

I know it's expensive but you'll be able to split it soon to get more plants.
It may be big enough for your grandchildren to split when they grow up.

You'll need to give it a good soak before you plant it.
This plant has been lying on its side and has missed the watering can for weeks.

It shows a bit of character being this shape, doesn't it?
This poor little tree got mangled somewhere along the line. It's a wonder it's still alive.

On no account should you let the roots dry out.
The roots have dried out already.

Many customers will ask for something to put their
purchases in. This is extremely inconsiderate.

Would your children like to go and watch the cows in that field?
Any chance of getting your brats out of the selling area? They've
smashed three flowers off already.

*It starts flowering in May and goes on blooming gloriously all
summer.*
It flowers in May and occasionally produces another bloom or two
just before the end of October.

This is one of the earliest to flower.
Year after year this plant will have its bloom ruined by late frosts.

We've completely sold out of it – it went like a bomb.
We only managed to grow three and are kicking ourselves for not
having grown three hundred.

It won't grow on your soil.
I've only got a few left and I'm damned if I'm letting you have one
of them.
or
I know you won't be able to keep it alive and I don't want your
complaints when it dies.

It is important to remember that despite the vicissitudes of dealing
with nurseries – trekking out to their premises, working in with
their odd opening hours, waiting patiently, sometimes for years,
for orders and having to deal with lots of different firms – they are
the only way of building up a first-rate collection of plants. Some
nurserymen, those with a touch of egocentricity about them,
hanker after the media and become popular personalities.

The Media Gardener

Media experts come from various backgrounds. Some are very
soundly educated in their field and are entertaining personalities
too. Others are, well, different. There are several approaches to
handling fame and fortune and most gardening personalities adopt
a kind of earthiness to reassure their audience that they are
everyday amateurs, just as crummy at gardening as the rest of us.
Radio experts are inclined to be dry, plain-speaking and a touch

humourless. On programmes where a panel of them is asked by the audience for advice, they answer the same questions every week. The questioners always sound the same too. In fact, the only change seems to be the venue. To become a really famous personality, you have to get on to TV.

If you are intending to become a gardening expert yourself, it will not be absolutely necessary for you to appear on television frequently. An occasional airing of your garden at the hands of one of the regulars will do nicely. When this happens, you won't be allowed to say too much because the media lads (and lasses) have a deep-seated fear of being upstaged. The procedure is usually as follows: the programme presenter will actually conduct you round your own garden, showing you places and plants you didn't know you had. While this goes on, three giant lorries will have parked on your lawn and a team of about 60 technicians will be cavorting about among the priceless treasures of your little scree garden. They all have size twelve shoes.

To add to the bedlam, a crowd of neighbours and camp followers is turning up to have a good gawp. You'll overhear acquaintances uttering remarks like:

'Can't think why they want to film *her* garden, unless it's for a murder or something', or 'I suppose the programme's been running so long they've run out of decent gardens to show.' Some of them will lurk about, adopting odd poses and reciting little gems of gardening knowledge. These people are hoping, in some way, to be used as extras. (Everyone wants to be on telly.)

At this stage, if you want to build up the crowd a bit, you earmark your most voluble neighbour and mutter, 'We can't really get going until Terry gets here,' and you leave it at that, although you might add a knowing wink. Very soon the rumour is through the crowd and people look hopefully into every passing car in the hope of being the first to glimpse Terry Wogan arriving on the scene. A while later, your neighbour sidles up to you again.

'No sign of Terry yet,' he whispers.

'He's over there', you reply, 'handing round those polystyrene beakers of tea.'

'Who is?'

'Terry Cotter. Our Youth Training lad. He wants to go into television so we couldn't really start without him. Wouldn't be fair.'

Once the filming begins in earnest you have to keep on your toes because time is of vital importance and the producer gets into the most frightful bate if it all goes wrong. Furthermore, it invariably begins to rain as soon as the cameras have started shooting. You are asked to show why and how you planted up various bits of your garden and while the presenter tells you your answer, the cameras take close-up shots of the technicians' size twelve feet.

If you have a very large garden, some of the more energetic presenters may want to crash about through your shrubbery pretending to be plant hunting in Nepal. This fashion has crept in since being pioneered on the small screen by people like David Attenborough, and can be pretty realistic, even in a garden in the Bristol suburbs. The technique is as follows: the cameras get set up and the presenter climbs to the top of a middle-sized oak. At the word ACTION! he leaps straight onto the rhododendron growing at its base. He straightens up, beams into the camera and says, breathlessly:

'Boy! Fancy finding such a su*perb* example of *Rhododendron thomsonii* here. The last one I fell into was in Sikkim when I was a lad. Imagine the thrill Sir Joseph Hooker must have had when he introduced it in 1849.' He manages to say all this without wavering, which is quite an achievement because, on the way down, he has practically neutered himself on one of the oak's branches. He only loses control when the cameraman says the shot was no good because a twig got stuck over the lens. As the presenter assumes you've never been to Nepal, you won't have been invited to take part in this bit, but it certainly pays to do a quick check for tigers after the crew have left the premises. With the need for realism on television, you never can tell!

When the ordeal is over and the crew have all repaired to the pub to fill out their expense claim forms, you will be left with a few broken plants and a good number of tyre tracks in your lawn. But don't despair. It will all have been worthwhile because you are well on the road to becoming a true recognised garden expert.

When is that programme going out? Friday? You'd better get some extra food in. You'll be under seige from admiring fans all weekend. What? Hadn't you realised? Oh yes, you can expect about 1,500 visitors on Saturday.

The Floral Artist

A good deal of what has already been said about garden experts applies to the Floral Artist. Plants which are good for floral art are often unsuitable for a garden, and a flower arranger's garden will usually contain some very peculiar-looking specimens. Plants with gross abnormalities like twisted stems or de-pigmented leaves are especially popular almong FAs. For example, there is a kind of hazel whose growth hormones are in disarray and which, as a result of this disease, produces horribly contorted trunks and stems. You'll find one of these psychotic hazels in every FA's garden.

FA's are full of all kinds of technical knowledge about how to make things last in water, how to preserve leaves for winter, which colours look right together, which vases are suitable for which flowers, and so on. Floral art, like cooking, is a transient art form. As much work and artistry goes into a major flower arrangement as Mozart might have put into an operatic aria, but the best preservatives in the world won't make the arrangement last anything like as long as *'Là ci darem la mano'*.

This is inclined to make many FAs rather melancholy, a characteristic which deepens to masochism when it comes to having your work judged at competitions. There are those who think the flower arrangement tent at Chelsea has a three-mile queue because so many people want to see the arrangements. Not true; they want to gloat over the cruelly damning remarks the judges have left on their little white cards. The only competitor to escape this public humiliation is the winner of the first prize. For the rest it's straight to the jugular: 'Nice arrangement spoilt by a lack of sensitivity about the container', or, 'Wrong colour backcloth and your chrysanths are rather bunched', or, 'Unfortunate use of textures. Rather formless.' These remarks, and many more cruel, are there for all to see. And after you've slaved on your arrangement for days, and spent weeks before that thinking out your line and form!

FAs are also inveterate jackdaws. Where a lesser person would step over a rotting piece of bark in a wood, or an oddly shaped fir-cone, or a stone with hole in it, the FA will shout, 'Ooh lovely, an *objet trouvé*, just what I wanted for floral club next week.' FA's houses have whole cupboards of such oddments.

If a village ever decides to have a floral festival, it is always necessary to enlist the services of a chief FA. Once in charge, she will recruit a group of henchwomen and form a kind of junta. During this time nothing in your garden is safe; anything could be requisitioned, from a potted orchid to a Georgian well head.

Now you have surveyed a few of the main types of expert, it is time to plan your move into the realms of horticultural brilliance. Here are some simple exercises to get you started on the road to fame.

1 Go out and buy a faded old Panama hat. If you can't find one, try a sports shop and buy a floppy cricket hat. Leave it overnight on weak tea and for a week in the dog's basket. Then, after washing it, wear it at all times. Committed garden experts can have the hat surgically attached, but be careful; the operation may be irreversible.

2 Nip outside and count up the plants in the flower bed nearest your back door. This will enable you to say, truthfully: 'We've begun cataloguing our plant collection.'

3 Go to your local estate agent and find out what your house is worth. Buy a copy of *Country Life* to see what crumbling manors are on the market. Then buy *The Grower* magazine. You'd be surprised how many 'specialist' nurseries seem to be for sale. Does this tell you anything?

4 If you see, growing amongst the flowers in your garden, a sow thistle, do you **(a)** pull it out; **(b)** study its morphology; **(c)** pull the flowers out to give it more room; or **(d)** you wouldn't recognise a sow thistle if it leapt up and bit you.

If your answers are (a), (b) or (c), go on reading this book. You have the necessary preoccupation with growing things. If your answer is (d), you must also go on reading this book because you need to learn what you're up against.

Chapter 2

Talking the Lingo

'It's wrote 'oggins but tha' is asrais'.'

(Quote from local man delivering sand and gravel)

Throughout Britain, Newcastle, PPLO and Fatty Liver-Kidney Syndrome were all endemic. Hitchener 'B' strain was used for the former but the role of biotin in the latter was not fully understood until the mid-1970s. By then, in the United Kingdom, the policy of using a dead vaccine for Newcastle had long been abandoned.

If you are a chicken farmer, or a veterinarian, you will have a good idea about what the foregoing means. It's not from any text – I just made it up – but it sounds mysterious and has just enough about it to attract the interest of any like-minded soul. To be an acknowledged gardening expert, you will need to have a similar skill, that is, to speak the right language.

Everybody is multilingual. Those who can handle conversations in French, German or Swahili – or all three – may be few, but within our own tongue we have quite a range of different languages. The curse of Babel is just as effective within one nation as it is across the world. 'Gentlemen lift the seat' says the notice. Is this a statement? – for they certainly do – or is it an exhortation? – 'Gentlemen! Lift the seat.' Clearly, both meanings are correct in this case because the notice refers only to gentlemen and, equally clearly, members of the male sex who are not gentlemen do not lift the seat.

English is especially good for misinterpretation, so everyday life is full of misleading statements. On Underground escalators, for instance, it says: 'Dogs must be carried', but supposing you haven't got a dog? Must you then go down the emergency stairs?

An 'off-licence' means the place *is* licensed to sell booze. A 'level crossing' is usually anything but level; a 'critically acclaimed' book is one the critics liked but nobody else could understand, and so on.

Then there are dialects. Each person has his own special range. There's familyspeak – some families use their own words, usually from obscure and inexplicable origins, for everyday things. In familyspeak you can say things like: 'Be a lamb and pop the tweakers in the bopper or we'll never get a slump', and be clearly understood by your partner. Jobspeak, especially among young aspiring professionals, is a skill that has to be learnt early on in their careers if they are to succeed. Recruiting advertisements are full of phrases like 'interpersonal skills', 'dedicated high achiever' and 'director level experience'. Listen to young professionals in a train and you'll hear words like 'handsonmanagement', 'moneyupfront' and 'userfriendly' being used again and again. Nobody has a wireless in his car these days. It's called 'in-car entertainment'. Really high-powered executives have 'in-car IT' (information technology – 'phones to the rest of us). With air travel costing so little these days, most people need to have a smattering of American, even if they can't be fluent. One should at least know the American for everyday words. In the States, for example, unpaid drudges are called 'homemakers'. A clever arse who is pig ignorant is called a 'sophomore'. (In England such people are called marketing experts.) Finally, and this is the bit that concerns *you*, there is hobbyspeak.

Hobbyspeak is a language designed to keep the doors closed to outsiders. Sailing, golf and anything to do with horses are well known for their impenetrable terminology. When it comes to gardening, there is not only jargon but a wonderful array of scientific terms that will make almost everyone who isn't a thorough expert feel utterly inferior. All plants have a scientific name – sometimes two or three – and these are changed with bewildering frequency, so, as soon as you are used to one particular handle, it will become something else. Occasionally the same name is given to more than one plant. But the jargon doesn't end here. There are not only scientific names for parts of plants, for techniques, for diseases and disorders and for equipment used, there is also a mass of difficult colloquial and semi-colloquial terminology which will crop up in every gardening conversation.

The secret of success with this language barrier is to learn to use a small amount of knowledge effectively and not to worry too much about getting things dead right. Nobody, not even the top botanists, ever gets everything right and part of the fun of being a garden expert is arguing the toss over whether, say, a particular plant is *Cyclamen cilicicum* var. *intaminatum* or *C. Cilicicum* 'Alpinum'. The aim of this chapter is to equip you with the necessary smattering of knowledge so that you'll be up there with the best of them, warbling away in dog Latin and throwing in an obscure Anglo-Saxon term whenever seems appropriate. After all, if you want to be a garden expert, it doesn't really matter what you say, as long as it sounds impressive.

Before going into detail, I must stress the importance of studying other experts. TPs are especially worth while. Just lurking in the bushes to watch them in action is better than taking a degree course. Imagine yourself up to your neck in a *Prunus lusitanica* deep in some fancy garden like Knightshayes. A couple of TPs are approaching. It sounds almost like a game of chess:

TP one (White plays to KKt4, a weak move which does very little development and puts a pawn on a square where it is not useful yet)*: 'That's a rhododendron isn't it? That big shrub showing white through the trees?'
TP two (Black replies P to K4, a reasonable move developing some pieces and occupying a good square): 'Rhododendron? Flowering in September?'
TP one (White then plays a perfectly horrible move, P to KB3): 'Could be *diaprepes*. That's late. Or its hybrid "Polar Star".'
TP two (Black replies Q to R5): '*Diaprepes* isn't especially late. You're thinking of *auriculatum* – the other parent. Besides, the hybrid is "Polar Bear". There is no such variety as "Polar Star". Anyway,' TP two continues, 'if you look carefully through the trees you'll see that it's nothing more special than a white hydrangea, *paniculata,* I'd say. Probably *paniculata* "Grandiflora", though it's hard to tell from this distance, of course.' (Queen is delivering a check to which there is no answer.)

*Lifted from Gerald Abrahams, *Teach Yourself Chess*,
E.V.P., 1962.

The Naming of Plants

You need to know how and why plants are named the way they are. 'Why can't they have ordinary English names?' people ask, as they try to get their tongues round impossible genera like *Schlumbergera* or *Eschscholzia*. The answer is simple. Anyone could use them if they were. The chief culprit, who started all this Latin business, was a Swedish genius called Carl von Linne. He even latinised his own name to Linnaeus. Anyway, in the middle of the eighteenth century, this Linnaeus chap sent out a decree across all the land that all God's creatures shalt have a binomial system of naming. Sweden being, then as now, the world's number one superpower, he persuaded the rest of the world to adopt his system. Every plant and animal was henceforth required to have a generic name – to begin with a capital letter – and a species name – to begin with a small letter.

Linnaeus himself took this binomial naming system to ridiculous extremes, even giving his books titles that looked like genus and species: *Systema plantarum* and *Genera naturae,* for example. As you can see from the titles, the books were not exactly bodice rippers, but they were pretty important in the annals of botanical science.

Once given this system, the later botanists and experts did the rest. Everyone wants immortality, so the race was on to name a plant or animal after oneself. Common names like Smith and David (*smithiantha* and *davidia*) were soon used up and it became necessary for more difficult surnames to be put to use. Nobody regarded Japanese or Chinese gardeners very seriously in those days – after all, they'd only been at it for about 8,000 years longer than we had – so, luckily, we in the West did not have to learn how to write names in Chinese characters. Camellias and China roses were just called that and not 山茶花 and 中国玫瑰. Now who's complaining about Latin names?

The joy of the international naming system is that it's all so fluid and changeable that nobody really knows which names to use. Botanists keep ringing the changes and nurserymen keep wringing their hands. They usually change the names too, but lag well behind, altering their catalogues just before the botanists go for yet another reclassification.

The joy of the international naming system.

As an expert, all you need do is sound convincing and have a goodish knowledge of some universal terms. That way you can learn to mix a little erudition with a lot of bluff. The golden rules are:

1 Never correct yourself once you've given a plant a name. If someone else corrects you, hit back by saying: 'Oh, you're still calling it that are you?'

2 Whenever you're told the name of a plant, look inscrutable and say, 'Mm'.

3 Never use English for anything except an English variety; French, Arabic or Chinese colloquial names are fine. Also, always use the foreign variety name if you can. The roses 'Scarlet Fire' and 'Iceberg', for example, should really be called 'Scharlachglut' and 'Schneewittchen', as they were raised by a German breeder.

A good many species names are descriptive and it is useful to have translations handy of some of the more commonly used ones. Understanding them helps, but, more important, if you know what the word means, you can apply it to plants you cannot otherwise identify. Here is a little glossary to help you.

albopilosum White-haired. Refers to True Plantsmen.
barbata With red-and-white striped stems.
brewerana Plants that yield juices suitable for fermenting into alcohol.
campestre Of fields – suitable to pitch a tent under.
candidum About to stand for Parliament.
cashmiriana Plants bearing soft wool-like substance of great value.
chinensis Can be taken away or consumed on the premises.
coronaria Belonging to the Queen. Commoners may not grow these plants.
crispa Dead or dead-looking.
cyaneus Extremely poisonous.
depressus Brassed off.
elatior Happy, excited.
elegans Modish, fashionable.
fallowiana To do with deer.
fulgens Red faced.
glomerata Get knotted.

grandiflora Suitable for use in five-star hotel foyers.

humilis Creepy.

hepatica see **icterina.**

icterina see **hepatica.**

isophylla American-style cocktails.

italica Flowers slope to the right.

lactiflora Thrives as well on dairy products as on margarine.

longissima Pertaining to after-dinner speakers.

leylandii Pertaining to buses.

maritima Ocean-going.

millefolium Kind of flaky pastry filled with cream and jam.

montana A United State.

narcissiflora Dies unless grown near a mirror or still water.

nudicaule Raised by a naturist society.

nutans see **brewerana.**

nuttallii Bears all known nuts.

obtusa Unintelligent.

officinalis Government-approved.

paniculata Suitable for frying.

pseudonarcissus Pretends to love itself.

pubescens Can't make up its mind whether to be a short alpine or a tall perennial.

purpureus Any plant that appears in a passage from literature often quoted in schools: 'rosemary for remembrance', 'oxlips and the nodding violet', etc.

pyramidalis Discovered in an ancient Egyptian tomb.

repens see **humilis**

reticulata With handbag.

sargentiana As discovered by a famous plant collector who was also a senior NCO in the Indian Army.

saxatile Pertains to jazz musicians.

stolonifera Originally slang, but now in regular use. It means 'nicked'.

sylvestris Introduced by a 1950s dance band.

tinctoria Partial to an occasional dram. Water only with whisky.

tremula Afraid.

tuberhybrida Bearing flowers shaped like sousaphones.

verticillata Little sugary bits that go on top of cakes.

vinifera see **brewerana.**

Once you have memorised a handful of these basic species names, you are half-way along the road to inventing your own plant names. Getting the genus right may look easy, but it isn't. The world is littered with plants masquerading as something different. There are senecios pretending to be ivies, shrubs that look exactly like holly until they produce a crop of exotic flowers, and even anemones that look a bit like daisies. If it looks like something fairly familiar, don't be fooled into calling it by a genus you already know. The safest bet is to invent a completely new name for the time being. Think of a very unusual surname. Preferably one with an odd spelling, add a suitable Latin-sounding root and then tack on the most appropriate species name. Suppose you observe a red-flowered bush growing in someone's garden. It may well be a something *fulgens,* so think up a surname – let's say Navratilova – you'll have to add a bit for latinisation and should say: 'Is that not *Navratilovaria fulgens?*'

'No, *Embothrium,*' says your host.

'Exactly. Just what I thought,' you reply, 'Re-classified now, of course. *Embothrium fulgens.*'

'*Coccinea*, actually.'

'Yes, yes, I meant *coccinea.* I always get that muddled – it's really more of a *fulgens* red than a *coccinea* red, don't you think?'

'Possibly.' And there you have the name to commit to memory without, you hope, having displayed your ignorance.

For some reason, horticulture abounds with names that beg misinterpretation. Some sound like diseases – *Glechoma hederacea* suggests a frightful affliction of the eyes and *Streptocarpus* sounds more like a sore throat bug than a South African native herb. The name *Sedum rhodiola* evokes, for me, a 1950s-style radiogram. One can imagine the advertising copy: 'Curl up and relax with the pure tones of the Sedum Rhodiola. Will play up to eight 78-rpm discs automatically. Beautiful simulated-walnut cabinet with teak knobs and magic eye tuning, all for £29.17s.6d.'

There are plenty of plant names that sound plain silly, but others can be very close to contravening the obscenity laws. The pine genus, *Pinus,* is sure to produce a crop of red faces, especially when pronounced in modern Latin pronunciation. *Pinus rigida* could have been more tactfully named. There was a cranesbill called *Geranium rectum album* which has thankfully been renamed *G. clarkii,* and a dreadful creeping ground cover plant called *Rubus fockeanus.* However it may sound, this has nothing to do with *Gaylussacia,* which is a huckleberry, or *Gaya* which is really *Hoheria.* There's a blue-eyed grass called *Sisyrinchium* 'Ball's Mauve', and a showy kind of bistort called *Polygonum bistorta* 'Superbum'. There's even a *Clematis alpina* cultivar with pink, drooping flowers called 'Willy'. As for that lovely tall-growing perennial lobelia – every garden should have it for its charming character and dependability, but nobody does because the botanists chose to dub the poor thing *Lobelia syphilitica.* You have to learn to reel off embarrassing names with complete aplomb. One stammer and you're done for.

Variety names can be infuriating. When they are named after people or places no problem arises. *Dicentra formosa* 'Langtrees' or *Brunnera macrophylla* 'Hadspen Cream' are straightforward names. But let the marketing experts loose on new varieties and you will be amazed at how inappropriate the naming can be. There is usually a tendency to use wet little sobriquets or to resort to superlative language. Either way, most variety names will set your teeth on edge. The dwarf iris 'Nylon Ruffles' sounds like the product of an underwear fetishist. Sweet pea 'Snoopea' is irritating, but *Ageratum* 'Pink Powderpuffs' really takes the biscuit. What about *Iris* 'Little Rosy Wings'? Pity they couldn't call it something simple like 'Murdoch'.

There are also some pretty nauseating common names. 'Baby's breath' for *gypsophila* was obviously coined by a childless person who had never experienced how foul a child's breath can be. Some bright herbert has decided to call *Alstroemerias* 'Princess Lilies' – who was Princess Lily anyway, Lily Langtry? Everything has to be 'naice and refained'. Cow-parsley is called 'Queen Anne's lace' in posh circles but Lincolnshire country folk call it 'kek'. So did Shakespeare (read *Henry V*) and, anyway, kek seems a more apt name for the beastly stuff.

There is a special language for describing plant varieties. Words like 'dainty' and 'unusual' crop up a lot. Anything with flowers that hang downwards is called 'nodding'; tubular flowers are always 'trumpet' shaped. Displays are 'stunning' or 'dazzling'. Dull plants have 'subtle qualities' and ugly plants are said to be 'full of character'. After a while these terms will trip easily off your tongue.

Pronunciation

If you still want to be a plant and garden expert you will need to work quite hard at developing your pronunciation. There is not really a right or a wrong way to pronounce most names, but this whole area depends on your personal inclinations. It's a bit like the toilet versus lavatory argument. 'Toilet' types are likely to pronounce some plant names differently from 'lavatory' folk. You must decide which ball park suits you, but, whatever you decide, you can be sure that the way you pronounce certain plant names will tend to classify *you* as well as the plants.

In his book *Clematis,* Christopher Lloyd has a whole chapter on names, spelling and pronunciation. It is a delightful piece of snobbery (although correct spelling is essential) and in no way devalues a first-rate reference book which is a joy to read as well as being excessively valuable to anyone who grows clematis. Nevertheless, those people who pronounce the plants clem*ay*tis are also likely to say 'toilet', to hold their knives and forks like pencils and to call napkins 'serviettes'. People who wear silk headscarves knotted on their chins, call jacks on playing cards 'knaves' and dine in the evening rather than 'get' high tea, are likely to call the plant clematis (as in clemency). You will need to know the differences in approach so that you can score points by correcting your friends' pronunciation. There are several golden rules which, once learnt, will stand you in good stead.

1 Whenever a name is foreign, try to get the pronunciation right for the language. The rose 'Maigold' is mostly called 'Maygold' in England but you should try to pronounce it in German if you can: 'Mygolt'. The scented *rugosa* rose 'Roserie de l'Hay', which most people call 'Rosery de lay', should sound like 'Rroserie de Lie' – try making a nice gutteral French 'r' and keep the syllables short and clipped. Now try 'Blanc Double de Coubert' – go on, read it out loud: 'Blonc dooble de coobairr'. Well done! that's coming on very nicely.

2 With Latin names, try to go for the most natural sound. You'll soon find out that clematis is the exception and that most plant names have the stress on the second or third syllable. If you want to be a real maverick, try a completely new approach. But be sure

you use the same pronunciation every time. Lack of consistency will soon show and your credibility will slide.

3 Make a special effort to deal with the most difficult names by practising them in the privacy of your bathroom. *Paeonia mlokosewitchii* baffles almost everyone. The most hardened expert usually chickens out on this one, feebly resorting to the nickname 'Molly the Witch'. The trick is to forget the first syllable. *Ligularia przewalskii* is another good one. Unless you are Polish, a batch of consonants at the beginning of a word is frightening. The point is, you don't pronounce them at all. Just ignore them, so that the 'P' in *przewalskii* is silent as in Psmith. Say 'Zeworskii' and you'll impress everyone except the Eastern Europeans. After all, if Lech Walesa is pronounced 'Leff Wowainsa', what hope is there for the rest of us?

If you take care to study all of this language in action, you'll soon get the hang of it. You must also learn to recognise the different types of floral dialect. Here are a couple of examples, heard from inside a bush at Sissinghurst. First, two members of the Slowlews Chippings Women's Institute:

'In't we got a nice day for it, Hilda!'

'Mm. Shame about the heat though, Pearl. I was ever so uncomfortable on the coach.'

'Never mind, dear. Now, what's that lovely pink thing?'

'I think that's what we used to call lady in the bath when I was a girl. *Dicentra* something . . . I don't think I'll be able to go far today.'

'Why's that, dear? It's ever so dainty, in't it?'

'Unusual, I call it. 'Cos my leg's swelling. It's the heat. Look at them clemaytis, growing out o' them urns.'

'Is it yer operation, dear? What's that underneath the clemaytis? Ooh look, busy lizzies. Aren't they early with them? Look at that one – that's a real cerise that is. Just like our Susan's new Fiesta. Ooh mind, 'ilda. There's nasty steps here.'

'I don't think I'll be able to manage them, Pearl. I had twenty-seven stitches, remember.'

'I'll help. What's them things growing at the bottom? Why so many?'

'Why so many what?'

'Stitches.'

'I'm sure I don't know. Ooh yes. They look like what we used to call angel tears.'

'Don't be daft, 'ilda. Angel tears is miniature daffs, they'd be over by now. Anyway, Elsie never 'ad that many.'

'Never 'ad that many what? Daffs?'

'Naoh! Stitches, silly! Anyway, I don't mean *them* angel tears, they're whossname . . . *Triandus* something. No, I means them pinky purple thing like glads.'

'Like Glad's whats?'

'Oh go on with yer. Like gladdies. Did you know she'd broken her hip?'

'Who?'

'Glad, 'oo else was we talking about?'

'We wasn't. You was telling me about angel stitches or something. Oh, now I know what you mean. Angels' fishing rods. We saw them at that place in Devon. Come on, Pearl, let's get a cup of tea. These shoes are killing my feet.'

'That'll be nice. You can tell me about your leg. When was it you 'ad yer operation?'

'Nineteen forty seven.'

Later, from inside the same bush, two smart middle-aged persons are overhead bumping into each other:

'Cynthia! Darling! Fancy meeting you here!'

'Air hairlair Jeremy. Thought you'd be in the City.'

'Just been down to Lamberhurst. Seeing a client. My dear! Have you seen the crowds!'

'Nair. Croids bore me. I'm looking at the plants. Aren't they heaven?'

'Me too, darling! Utter heaven! Done the cottage garden yet?'

'Ra*ther*. Those divine colours. What's that pretty vetchy thing with orange flowers?'

'*Lathyrus aureus.*'

'What? used to be *Orobus?* But that's pink.'

'Different species. Do you recognise that lime greeny thing in the woody bit?'

'Oh that's a weed. *Smyrnium perfoliatum.* Daddy planted it at Meubles years ago. Been an absolute curse ever since.'

'Not garden-worthy?'

'Absolutely not.'

'By the way. Down in the herb garden. Orris.'

'Who the hell's Horace?'

'No, orris. You know, *Iris florentina.*'

'What about it?'

'I'm mad on the stuff. Know where I can get any?'

'Oh certainly. We've got scads of it. All over the banks at Meubles. Why not come up this weekend and I'll get Soames to dig you a barrowful.'

'Cynthia. You're an absolute brick! I say, let's give you a kiss.'

'Oh do push orf, Jeremy! Besides, it's not Cynthia. It's Celia if you really want to know.'

'Air. How *frightfully* embarrassing!'

After a while, you will find Latin names flitting off your tongue with ease. Once this happens, other experts will begin to take notice of what you say. You will be said to be *knowledgeable.* 'Knowledgeable' doesn't mean having a wide understanding of things horticultural. Many gardening journalists are highly knowledgeable but couldn't grow a row of peas to save their lives. 'Knowledgeable' simply means being able to trot out a string of well-pronounced technical names for plants without hesitation. Accuracy's no problem. You don't need it.

Adding a word or two about origin helps enormously. If you know exactly where a plant came from, when it was introduced and by whom, it always pays to say so. If you're a bit vague about this, have a stab anyway, but keep it general. Occasionally the name will give you a clue: it's unlikely that *Verbena peruviana* came from Australia, but don't bank on it being Peruvian. You should say something like, 'Oh how I love *Verbena peruviana,* in fact I'm into all New World genera.' A lot of our garden plants came from China, Nepal or somewhere in the Asian mountains. Anything '*virginiana*' is probably a Tradescant introduction dating back to his transatlantic jaunts in the seventeenth century. Anything '*douglasii*' probably comes from North America too.

Although it goes a long way to making you an expert, being well versed in scientific nomenclature isn't quite enough. There are a number of jargon terms which you must master if you are to have a thorough understanding of gardening language. Here, as in Latin, you can invent a certain amount. A number of terms are local, with different meanings in different parts of the country. This can result in something similar to the battle of wits one always has to have when trying to buy a loaf of bread in a strange town.

'Good morning sir, how may I help you?' Well, let's try to keep this within the bounds of possibility. The shop girl's opening utterance is more likely to be:

'Huh?'

'I'd like a cottage loaf, please.'

'We 'aven't got no cottage loaves.'

'They're just behind your left ear, next to the milk loaves.'

'Milk loaves?'

'Those round squashy things.'

'What these?' She prods a black fingernail deep into one of the loaves in question.

'Yes.'

'They're bloomers.'

'OK, bloomers. Now will you pass me one of those cottage loaves.'

'I told ya, we ain't got no cottage loaves.'

'Well what do you call those round things.'

'Coburgs.'

'Oh, coburgs. And an iced bun please.'

'Swiss bun.'

'And I think I'll have a few crumpets.'

'Crumpets?'

'Those disc-shaped –'

'Do wha'?'

'Sorry. Them round things whot've got holes.'

'Pikelets.'

'And the same to you, young lady!'

If you ever employ the services of a faithful old gardener you are likely to suffer a similar language barrier. This won't matter too much because faithful old gardeners always know best and never do what they're told anyway. Some will go out of their way to obstruct you and even the most benign are as wilful as toddlers and a great deal more destructive. Matters are always worse if you are new to an area, particularly if you have bought the local crumbling manor or rectory. Buildings of this type frequently come with a trusty old soul who will arrive on an ancient bicycle and talk gibberish.

'The kitchen garden seems a bit overgrown,' you might say.

'Ooh! Aah! That wants more'n just a bit o' petherin.'

'I thought we'd plant potatoes – to clean the ground.'

'Niver 'appen!'

'Sorry?'

'Tain't never tate land. S'too clarty.'

'Well, what do you suggest?'

'S'up to you, really.'

'But what would *you* do?'

'Git rid o'nt.'

'But it's an ancient kitchen garden. It must have produced food for the house for a hundred years or more.'

'Ooh aah.'

'So why not now?'

'Sick soil.'

'Sick?'

'Aah. Tain't no good for nothing now, only twitch and bellbine.'

All this really means that he is damned if he's going to break his back forking the couch grass out of the vegetable beds or double digging, or any other strenuous stuff. However, if you're looking for someone to trim your edges, dead-head a few roses, train a dozen sweet peas a year and drink gallons of your Nescafé on interminable breaks, he's your man. When you have slipped a disc and developed a couple of hernias pulling the kitchen garden round to its original fertile and productive state he will (a) take all credit for the transformation, and (b) feed his and several other families on what he filches. You'll be left with cabbage and turnips while the rest of the village enjoys *petits pois,* asparagus and fresh raspberries.

One way to get the better of such a character is to have a good understanding of some of the jargon he uses and to baffle him with more that he doesn't. To help you with this, a short dictionary of terms suitable for gardening experts follows:

alternate leaves Only produces leaves every other year.

aphid Sucking insects which have the extraordinary ability to reproduce thousands of their own kind without sex. They carry viruses from one plant to another and are generally pretty bad news. Ants and ladybirds adore them so if you try to kill them with insecticide you'll kill their predators too, and compound

Faithful old gardeners always know best and
never do what they're told anyway.

your problems. There are insecticides that are allegedly harmless to non-aphids, but these are pretty harmless to aphids too.

apiary Simian behaviour peculiar to individuals who discover a live bee down their shirt-front. They are said to beat their chests in the manner of male gorillas.

aviary A make of scales especially designed for weighing caged birds when some are perching and others are on the wing.

barbecue A form of ancient sacrifice. Meat is burnt on an altar to induce instant heavy rain. Remarkably successful it is too.

bonfire A device to destroy your neighbour's garden party with smoke. Ought to be called a malfire really.

brishook Sickle – as in brishook cell anaemia, hammer and brishook, etc.

broadcast Spreading manure about. What every garden expert would like to do but very few actually manage on a nationwide basis.

bulb Not a corm.

clarty Thick, sticky and unyielding. Many old country gardeners are clarty.

chard A small market town in Somerset noted for its leaf vegetables.

coir Old word for church musicians who play their instruments behind the font on a special coconut fibre mat.

corm Not a bulb.

crab A marine apple with nippers.

die-back Anglicised form of the Welsh expression 'Dai, bach!' which means 'things are really settling down for winter just now are they not?'

fasciation Hideously squashed together stems caused by a malfunction in the growing tip at some stage in the plant's history. Some floral artists actually prize such abnormalities.

friable Suitable for deep or shallow pan.

frost mould Wonderfully friable soil produced by the action of deep frost on the newly dug clods. This disappears with the first heavy rains of March, leaving you with the cold, wet clay you first dug in autumn.

furnish Ordinary gardeners let vigorous climbers grow over stumps or fences. Posh gardeners 'furnish' their walls with wall plants.

graft 1. Hard, honest work. 2. Bribes.

heavy plant crossing A special point on major roadworks where large specimens of shrubs and trees can be carried across the road safely and legally.

hedging 1. A method of backing several horses but still winning. 2. A way of blotting out undesirable neighbours.

humus Something to be built up by adding anything that is otherwise quite undesirable and usually smelly to your soil. Excrement, rotting vegetation, dead tree bark and even kitchen waste can all be used to build up humus.

island bed Invention of a famous East Anglian gardener to show off perennials to advantage. In practice they look unnatural and are awkward to mow round.

layering A way of propagating otherwise difficult plants. A stem is anchored to the soil with a weight, or pinned down with wire. Years later, when you've forgotten all about it, the layer takes root and throws up vigorous stems which overcrowd the parent. At this stage the new plant can be removed from the parent and transplanted to a new spot where it will die.

monocarpic Describing a one-car family.

mulch Posh gardeners shovel mulches on by the lorryload. The fashion is to use material like pine bark chips which invariably migrate from borders to lawn, or farmyard manure which dogs love to bring into the house.

nectary The bit the bee goes for.

obovate A talent for split-reed woodwind instruments.

pan 1. Hard, compacted soil under the surface. All pans must be broken to ensure drainage – see **friable.** 2. **alpine pan.** A vessel for making Swiss fondue.

pH A bit hard to describe really, but it's an estimate of the number of hydrogen ions per dollop of stuff and relates to acidity. All you need to know is that if your soil is pH 7 or more, you will not be into rhododendrons. More than 8 means you're on chalk or lime and less than 5 means you have a pretty bad acid rain problem in your area. Many upper-crust gardeners believe it impossible to create a garden unless your soil is acid. Lower gardeners throw lime about to improve their fertility.

pleach Literally to entwine or interlace. In garden terminology it has come to refer to trees that are lopped and mangled into unnatural shapes to 'enhance' the landscaping. Good examples can be seen at Hidcote, where trees have been butchered into large, perfect cubes on skinny legs, and at several important gardens where laburnums have been deformed to make tunnels which are thus decorated with the hanging yellow blooms for one week of the year, but are boring for the remaining 51.

pollinate To chatter in a raucous manner like parrots. Frequently done at judges' lunches – see Chapter 4.

potager A lahdidah name for an ordinary veg patch where South Kensington-style greens are grown in a jumbled mess rather than neat rows. Few really useful plants like carrots and swedes are grown but anything with a fancy name like Good King Henry, lambs lettuce or *mange touts* will be found there. Also red cauliflower, purple peas and yellow peppers – anything that is *chic* enough to adorn the pages of *House & Garden*. The potager owner doesn't pick produce, she revels in the concept.

potting shed The last place to look for a missing tool.

prune A dried plum.

Ruby Chard Daughter of Fred and Mabel Chard, inventor of the red-stemmed leaf vegetable beloved of potager freaks.

scarify To put the wind up someone.

scorzonera Weedy little roots like half-starved parsnips. Little nutritional value but popular with vegetable snobs and the hempen homespun set.

scree In nature, a stony mountainside covered with small stones. In horticulture, anything mulched with pea gravel, from a 10-in pot to an alpine meadow.

skerrit A rampantly invasive vegetable beloved of nineteenth-century cottages but now shunned, even by potager growers.

sphagnum Mossy substance invaluable to horticulture, orginally discovered in County Kildare, Ireland, by Pete Boggs.

tetraploid An even lower creation than tabloid – four times lower to be precise. (There are also much higher lifeforms such as haploid, Christopherloid, loidsbank, loidwebber, etc. It will be to your advantage to study them all.)

thrips One thrips, many thrips. Horrible little creatures that are almost invisible but devour greenstuff with gusto and crawl all over your skin, making your flesh creep.

topiary Excessive drinking.

tuber Large musical instrument. Gerard Hoffnung was a virtuoso.

urn A receptacle in which to grow begonias or fuchsias, or somewhere to store the ashes of a deceased relative.

vine eyes Excessively bloodshot eyes, especially where the condition has been brought on by topiary q.v.

wardian case A specially designed glass travelling case for carrying wardians.

By now you should be developing the beginnings of a decent horticultural vocabulary. Your next step is to start practising your new langauge. Start off with people you know fairly well. Select friends who are moderately interested but quite ignorant about most things to do with gardening. As your confidence grows you will be able to test your etymological muscle on more seasoned plantsmen. If you feel doubts rising in your mind, shrug these off with the sure knowledge that they are probably as unsure of their material as you are. Even the greatest come unstuck from time to time and hearing them drop themselves into the proverbial mulch can provide enormous satisfaction. Here are some exercises for you.

1 Make up a single sentence using all of the following words. (Here, first, is an example: words – pether, coir, fasciation, *Fagus nudicaule*; sentence – I had to pether the ground round my *Fagus nudicaule* and surround it with a coir mat to prevent fasciation.)

   (a) slag, ruby chard, prune, *pubescens, elegans*

   (b) topiary, *nutans*, island bed, *brewerana*, vine eyes

   (c) tetraploid, graft, brishook, monocarpic, pH.

2 Think up some likely names that will do for plants you do not recognise. Remember to use a fairly unusual surname. Examples might be: *Tugenhadtia longissima, Kjeldhalia nuttallii* or *Titchmarshia elegans*.

3 Find the glossary in the front of any decent plant book and learn as many of the difficult anatomical names as you can. When you know the difference between ovate and obovate leaves, you are ready for the world.

4 Start going to flower shows and to good gardens open to the public. The main reason for this is not, as you might think, to learn by looking at the plants and the gardens, but to give you the opportunity of eavesdropping on as many conversations as you can. You'll soon begin to recognise an expert by the cut of his jib.

Chapter 3

~~~~~~

Coping with Flower Shows

~~~~~~

'Tomatoes rank as vegetables.'

(Rule 27 of the Royal Horticultural Society Exhibition
Regulations 1984)

'Did you do Harrogate last year?'
  'No fear. Chelsea was enough for us. No ropes.'
  'Well you wouldn't would you, Beezley never got ropes until the
year before last.'
  'So 'ow come Jane got ropes first time round?'
  'Well, I suppose it's on account of 'er leg.'

This kind of chat goes on between veteran flower show
exhibitors, partly to communicate with each other but mainly to
confuse eavesdroppers. Now that you've had a chance to learn the
proper language in Chapter 2, you are ready to find out about
flower shows and how to deal with them.
  The flower show is as English as roast beef. Size and scope range
from Chelsea, where a quarter of a million people compete to see
how many of them can fit into a tent without knocking it over, to
small village affairs where, in bygone days, the girls all wore bright
summer frocks and the exhibits were eclipsed by the flowers on
their mothers' hats. Those were days of strawberry teas, taken at
leisure while a genteel brass band played softly in the background.
Many a swain's heart beat fast under his striped blazer as he doffed
his boater to the pretty girl at the tombola stall. The basic
principles are the same today except that it's all a bit shabby.
Nobody dresses up much – the young of both sexes (if there are
still two sexes) wear motorbike suits or jogging kit, the band has
been replaced by a disco, and the prizes have the same monetary
value as they did in the 1920s.

Being a flower show exhibitor is essential for oneupmanship and will give you access to the latest news on the horticultural inner circuit. TPs haunt shows everywhere, so it is very important, if you yearn for recognition as an expert, that you shimmy into their vision a few times to drop a name or a place. If you don't actually have any names to drop, try inventing a few. Remember never to invent titled names – they can be looked up! Always qualify the name you drop with a little phrase like '. . . Molly Figment, over at Much Fibbing Manor', or, 'you know Hardacre, the Pemberton rose expert'. You may be able to bluff like that for quite a while before you are found out.

You will also need to win some medals, and should try for at least one trophy. The medals are usually just printed on cards these days, although the RHS gives you a real metal one the first time you win. You will need the cards for pinning up in your study or potting shed – preferably a little lopsidedly, as if you didn't really care whether you'd won them or not. Almost everybody wins a medal of some sort at flower shows, but outsiders rate them much more highly than they deserve. Whatever you win, you can be sure of effusive congratulations from the public.

Where are the Best Shows?

The main thing to remember is that the biggest are not necessarily the best. Most of the small village shows take place in late summer when dahlias are at their loudest but everything else in the garden is as dead as mutton. On the other hand, Chelsea is so early in the season that practically everything shown has to be forced. Several weeks in a hothouse followed by a week in a dark tent is enough to put anyone off colour – think of going on a world cruise and then attending ten wedding receptions in five days and you'll know how the plants feel by the end of the show. No wonder the tall pale pink plant you liked at Chelsea turned out to be short and red when it flowered naturally in your garden!

Some of the finest flower shows outside London happen in the north of England. The Harrogate Spring Show takes place at the end of April. This would be an excellent time except that spring doesn't start in north Yorkshire until about the third week in June. It is always cold and usually wet. One year, the main marquee collapsed under the weight of snow. However, Yorkshire people are hardy souls and the showground soon fills up with noisy enthusiasts. You can tell the southerners at Harrogate – they're the ones who wear clogs and cloth caps, thinking they might blend in better. The true northerners wear thick, sensible tweeds, stout walking sticks and rubicund faces – Yorkshire beer is full of nourishment and rather moreish.

Watching relations between north and south can be interesting. What passes for good, honest plain speaking in Yorkshire would be called bloody rude in Hampshire. Southern finesse is considered cissy up north, and so on. When it comes to studying the exhibits, you soon find out that northern gardeners are pretty switched on. Because winds whistle across the Pennines at 60 miles an hour every other day, nothing taller than about 3 inches will survive for very long up there. Hence the obsession with alpines. The Alpine Garden Society really goes to town at Harrogate. They have a huge tent with yards and yards of immaculate plants all in scrubbed clay pots and all flowering magnificently. Southern alpine specialists seem to be a little more jolly but are not half so dedicated. Just listening to the way they communicate will teach you a terrific amount about the north-south divide.

Southern enthusiasts will greet each other with ebulliance: 'My dear! Heavenly to see you again. What *charming* saxifrages. Oh, and that *Paraquilegia,* you clever thing! How do you get it to flower so well?'

'Couldn't be easier. I just neglect it. Chuck a bucket of water over it if I remember!'

'Oh what fibs. I bet you've positively sweated blood over it. And the pot! Not a mark, not a blemish.'

'No, it's really not that difficult. What are you showing?'

'My dear, I've *nothing* – absolutely B-all. Rodney's been over in the States half the winter and one simply hasn't had time, what with David's book coming out before Christmas and you-know-who coming to visit the gardens and Dominic being called to the Bar and all.'

'My goodness, you *have* been busy.'

'Well, yes. All I could manage was that poor little gentian I found in Nepal last year.'

You can tell the Southerners at Harrogate –
they're the ones who wear clogs and cloth caps.

'Not the natural hybrid – the pale form of *Gentiana depressa*. I
didn't think it would flower so early without being forced.'

'Well, it's probably a fluke. Anyway, that's all I've got, so it'll
simply have to do. The pity of it is, it's only got thirty-eight blooms
on it.'

'Darling! A new introduction, thirty-eight blooms and collected
personally – you're bound to get best in show.'

'Pouf! I'll be lucky to get a highly commended.'

Northerners are far more serious and a good deal more outspoken:
'Eh up!'

'Eh up yerself.'

'What've yer got this time?'

'This.'

'What d'yer call that?'

'If thou doesn't know what tha' is, thou must be a' ignorant
booger!'

'I di'n't say I di'n't knaw. I asked what thou calls it!'

'Well what does thou call it?'

'Thou tell me.'

'*Primula* "Bewerley White".'

'Nay lad! "Bewerley Whites" is about twice that size. Anyroad
yon plant's cream, not white.'

'Well that's what it was when m'father grew it, and m'grand-
father – "Bewerley White".'

'Well don't blame me when yer get disqualified for wrong
labelling.'

'I won a first wi't booger last year. This very plant.'

'Aye, but they 'ad that prat from Orpington on't judges panel.
'Es dead now.'

'Who's replaced 'im?'

'Guess!'

Northerners are usually less well off than southerners and are
always much more careful with their money. In the home counties,
£50 notes are waved about gaily.

'I'm afraid I can't change that,' you say apologetically when one
is proffered in payment for a single alpine at £1.25.

'Oh not to worry. Give me five of them. What's that jolly pink
thing?'

'*Thymus* "Pink Chintz".'

'Isn't it a duck! I must have it.'

'One?'

'No, ten. I'd lose one.'

Northern transactions are usually less unrestrained: 'Ow much are the auriculas.'

'One pound.'

'What *each*?'

'They are named varieties.'

'I'll 'ave one. No not that one, *that* one. It's ready for splittin' . . . or do I really want one?'

'They are very nice plants.'

'Mm, but aren't they small! Haven't you got any bigger ones?'

'I'm afraid not.'

'Oh, I suppose I'll 'ave to make do wi' yon little plant.'

'Would you like a crowbar?'

'A crowbar?'

'To prise open your purse.'

'Cheeky sod! Go on then, gi'me that one. Do I get a free carrier?'

And when she opens her purse you don't exactly see moths fly out – it's been closed too long for them to have survived. It even has pre-decimal money in it – brass threepenny bits and a half crown. But you can be cheeky up there, whereas a southern swell would have complained to the committee about the crowbar remark.

One of the big joys of Harrogate, apart from the setting of the Spring Show in the valley gardens, is the rock garden exhibit. Great lumps of rock are built into magnificent alpine scenes with little streams, secret crevices out of which grow rare saxifrages or primulas, and gravelly screes planted up with thousands of tiny plants – all big on colour. Bulbs, not just daffodils and tulips, but exquisite little plants like dog's tooth violets, fritillaries, crocuses and scillas abound everywhere. The richness of variety is hardly surprising for these alpines come from all the mountain ranges of the world: gentians from the Himalayas, primulas from Europe, calceolarias from the Andes and penstemons from the Rockies. It is hard to believe that such fragile blooms could survive the vicious night frosts and blizzards of their natural environments. But you try growing them at home. The icy blasts of the Urals are one thing – damp English winters are quite another.

Beginning in early summer and following the season to harvest time in late July are the agricultural shows. Queen of these is the Royal Show, which happens in the West Midlands, usually coinciding with American Independence Day. Farming has less and less to do with these shows nowadays. There was a time when all the local Giles would don their Harris tweed, grab their shooting sticks and go to sweat it out while their animals were led into the ring for the annual obesity contests. While their husbands beefed about the price of beef with each other, their broad-beamed womenfolk would be rubbing bottoms in the Women's Institute tent, looking at the raspberry jam competition — 'She must have used Certo to get that set' – and casting expert eyes over the fruit cakes – 'Dot's have gone a bit sad as usual'. Animal feed compounders had marquees with tables and chairs so their farmer customers could add to their ample waistlines and bosoms by eating piles of cucumber sandwiches and fancy cakes. The tea always tasted of grass mowings and your chair always sank slowly into the turf so that you ended up with your chin on the table or fell over backwards depending on which legs sank deeper into the ground. To go to a show in anything other than tweeds and a buttonhole was quite unthinkable.

The Royal Show today is designed for two groups: tractor manufacturers and the urban residents of Greater Birmingham. The former set out their wares in the hopes of tempting farmers to swell their overdrafts and buy great 200-horsepower monsters: 'This model comes with computer, four-wheel drive, air conditioning, assistor ram and compact disc hi-fi, special show price £38,000.'

The latter go for a day in the 'country' which means sharing a few hundred square yards with fifty thousand other 'country' lovers, buying a few 'country' balloons, browsing through 'country' stalls that sell keyrings with your name on them or 'country' mugs with your name on them or special custom-made 'country' nameplates for your house – anything from 'Dunroamin' to 'Highgrove Estate'. In the main ring there are 'country' exhibits like the Dancing JCBs, Metropolitan police dog handling and rural parachute drops. There's plenty of good 'country' food to eat too: rural candyfloss, 'country' hamburgers and 'country' hotdogs – hunt followers call them hothounds (pronounced 'hothinds'). If you are really lucky, you might be able to enjoy a display from the very heart of the shires by the Red Arrows.

The flower show at the Royal is tucked away about a mile from the main entrance. You have to wade through all the rural industries stands to get there. You also have to run a gauntlet of wholesale wine merchants. They advance on you in a pincer movement from all sides and simply won't be put down, however nasty you are:

'Like to try some of our wine, sir?'

'No thanks, I'm a wine lover.'

'Come on, sir, it won't take a minute.'

'I only drink water.'

'Have you tried our German wines before, sir?'

'Yes.'

'Which ones did you like?'

'I didn't.'

'We've a whole new range this year, sir.'

'Sorry. I only drink Trockenbeerenauslese.'

'Then you're in luck, sir.'

'But this is Austrian. I only drink German Trockenbeeren-auslese.'

'How about some Italian?'

'No thank you. I've just had my radiator re-filled with Blue-col.'

'What about a nice Yugoslav Riesling?'

'No. I prefer my salad with a dash of vinaigrette – it's less acid.'

'Bull's Blood?'

'I don't see the necessity for swearing.'

But he's such an earnest man and you feel guilty for snubbing him. 'Oh all right, let's have a taste.' You sip a few tiny thimbles of different liquids – they always give you one that tastes filthy first so, after that, anything slips down like nectar and you leave half an hour later, slightly tipsy, having ordered six cases of wine and three bottles of special Armagnac that is only available through this particular merchant and was a snip at £25 a bottle because it is 25 years old and, after all, what's a pound a year?

OK! I know what you're thinking. What does all this wine and country show stuff have to do with being a garden expert? Well, nothing really, so back to the flower tent.

Once there, in your semi-inebriated state, you think you are suffering from an attack of *déjà vu*, which you are because all the faces behind the stands in the flower tent are the same faces you saw at Harrogate, at Chelsea and every few weeks at Vincent

Square. There are usually a lot of roses – mostly bowls of modern hybrids – and fewer alpines than at Harrogate. You will have resolved not to buy anything because July is a frightful time to buy plants and, anyway, you don't want to spend the rest of your day carrying a heavy bag. But you see a Phlomis you've wanted for years and a Penstemon variety that has evaded you for as long as you have been collecting. Eventually, two carriers in each hand, you stagger back to the main part of the show to watch the motorbike display. It isn't until much later, when you are half-way down the M1, that you realise you've left all your plants in the grandstand. The moral is, don't mix horticulture with country pursuits.

At the very bottom of the scale is the village garden fête. Some flower competitions go on at these functions, but nothing big enough for you to promote your career as an expert. Muscling in here could land you in the middle of a three-generation family feud that makes the Montagues and Capulets look like bosom friends, so tread carefully! The great thing is to get your garden to the standard that might encourage the parish to see whether they could hold their fête in it. The kudos and status associated with being host garden for the village is quite enormous and could lead to greater things like a television appearance or an invitation to judge the flower competition. In some villages, this privilege is valued as highly as the lordship of the manor and is handed down to successive occupants of the same garden. You need plenty of lawn space and mustn't mind about holes and scars made by the marquee and the stalls. Things to avoid are pony rides – the ponies will eat your roses and kick and bite as viciously as the toddlers. Anything that tends to make people rowdy – booze, coconut shies, topless waitresses or bottomless vicars – should be ruled out. Other sources of discord are baby shows – the mothers invariably fall out with the judges – and book stalls that sell nothing but Mills and Boon romances. Tombola is tiresome because the youngest cub scout always wins the bottle of whisky and the colonel, who loves his chota peg, always wins the Harpic. The greatest disaster that can befall an English village fête is a cold, wet afternoon. This truly makes for a fête worse than death. It can also cause lasting damage to your lawns.

How to Exhibit Successfully

Although by no means all plant experts end up with their own nurseries, those that do will have the kind of nursery that requires a stand at one of the shows. Even if you have no intention of exhibiting in your own right, however, the chances are that you'll want to be involved in one of the society exhibits, or, at the very least, put up a plant or two.

Sooner or later, it is essential for all true gardening experts to have exhibited at one of the London shows. The sooner you get there the sooner your star will rise. Key reasons for showing at Vincent Square are:

1 It is your route to Chelsea. You have to be invited there and they like you to serve an apprenticeship in the halls first.

2 All the nobs go. You will meet not only top gardeners and plantsmen, but also people of lesser importance – like cabinet ministers, royalty, captains of industry – who, though not themselves experts, may be of great help to you. Some, if you intend to sell plants, will become customers. Remember, the bluer the blood, the longer the interval between delivering the plants and getting paid.

3 The shows are in London. Everybody likes to get a spell in London. If you sold your London home to buy a crumbling manor house in which to start your nursery, you will be so homesick for the capital by now that any excuse for going back will do. The sad thing is you'll be so broke from paying all those unexpected bills to mend the house that you won't be able to eat or sleep in Town. It might be consoling to sponge off your friends who still live and work in the City, and who now earn half a million a year, but won't it be galling when they keep saying, 'Think what your old house in Swiss Cottage must be worth now!'

There are those who dislike hotels and have no friends in Town. Walking down to the hall early one morning after a restful night at my club, a van door opened in front of me, blocking my way, and a fellow exhibitor half fell onto the pavement.

'Morning Fred,' I said cheerily. 'Good Lord, you look awful.' His shirt was out at the back, his hair tangled and his eyes were as red as a fresh herring's. 'You look as though you've been in there all night,' I said.

'I have,' he said.

'But isn't that frightfully uncomfortable?'

'It is when I've forgotten my pillow. Had to use a bag of compost.'

'Where do you clean up and things?' I asked.

'In the hall gents,' he said. 'It's the "and things" I'm desperate for at the minute. If they don't unlock the doors and let us in soon I'll have an accident.'

To show successfully you'll need a versatile mind, a sense of humour and a strong back. Anything that can go wrong will, and it is most unlikely that your exhibit will bear any resemblance to your original plan. However, preparation is still the key to getting your act together. There are highly organised and efficient firms which have the labour and resources to lay on fancy exhibits all over the country. Then there are the little one-man outfits which, because they are doing everything from organising finance to making the tea, only have time for a modicum of preparation. You, as a newly fledged gardening expert, are likely to fall into this category. Don't let this make you feel inferior. Remember, people like you are the backbone of most flower shows.

If you are showing before June, you will need a heated greenhouse. Don't think you'll have much control over the plants – you won't. The scenario is something like this. You are intending to show in Westminster in mid-February. You thought you'd construct a little woodland scene using snowdrops, aconites, violets, primroses, anemones and things like that. You will put your primroses and violets in the greenhouse in November to bring them on. The other stuff will, you hope, be in bud outdoors and can be lifted. Given enough sunny days through January – you can depend on there being about one and a quarter – and your spring flowers will be a glorious sheet of colour and fragrance. The day they reach the peak of perfection will be two weeks before or two weeks after the show, depending on the weather. It's the same outdoors. Those snowdrops will either be finished or not up. One year I actually had to hack them out of the ground with a pickaxe.

Growing the stuff is only part of the job. Getting your fragile material down to Westminster, if you live a hundred miles or more away, can be something of a challenge. At first you'll probably try doing it in about ten car journeys. Peering at the road ahead when your view is hampered by 200 daffodil blooms can be tricky, so it pays to pack the front of the car with something misty and not too dense like gypsophila or pussy-willow catkins. That way, you can see the blue lights on the police car more clearly. A couple of shows like this and you decide to invest in a van. Naturally, you are new to the nursery game and need to watch your capital expenditure very carefully, so it will have to be quite an old van – well, an ancient one really – well, let's face it, a clapped-out wreck. Once you start shopping around for vans, you soon find out that they are usually not advertised in the paper. Furthermore, you get the impression that they've all been used for illegal or immoral purposes. When you park a car, however old, in a town parking space, people ignore you. But if it's a ten-year-old Transit van you can almost see their lips move as they memorise the number. Policemen lurk nearby muttering darkly into the tiny radios they have in their breast pockets these days, and the shiftiest individuals walking by in greasy jeans and cloth caps give a knowing wink or a 'Cheers mate!'

The other thing you soon learn about old vans is that nothing can ever be quite as completely clapped-out as a Bedford or a Ford with 2,000 miles on the clock. You have no way of knowing whether that particular clock has been wound back, or whether it's on its second or its third time round. The rattle of a simple man is nothing to the rattle of a snookered van! Roadtesting our first was a nerve-shredding experience. 'Only done fifty thousand,' our salesman assured us, 'used by one careful driver – a jobbing decorator as it 'appened.' A hundred yards up the road the accelerator stuck down and we shot into the high street at an alarming pace.

Like most cars, vans have four gears, but, unlike cars, they are all bottom. In first gear the engine screams while you creep forward at about half a mile a day. For motorway work there is a sort of fourth from bottom which enables you to reach a respectable speed – well, if cyclists were allowed on motorways they wouldn't find you were holding them up too much. Vans are designed so that the engine is actually inside the cab with you so you are able to appreciate the smells and the noise to perfection. Earplugs, gas mask and a comprehensively stocked tool box are essential equipment.

Once you've loaded your exhibition plants, the peat, the old gnarled logs you swiped out of the local wood, stone slabs for the pathway, watering can, labelling equipment, tree branches, picnic lunch, suitcase, posh suit for evenings and half a ton of green moss, your van is groaning at the springs and you are ready for the off. You decide to take it easy, getting used to handling it loaded. Soon you realise why other van drivers always give the impression of being suicidal. You can see your way ahead clearly and the wing mirrors give you a little rear vision, but there are huge areas of complete blindness. Approach an oblique junction and you are done for. You have to creep out and hope. This problem is awkward on country roads; on Hyde Park Corner it is lethal. By the time you've got to Vincent Square you've also found out why most vans are covered in dents.

Trembling with a mixture of exhaustion and fear, you find your way to the Horticultural Hall. Along Elverton Street, which runs down the side of the hall, there are four parking meters, an army barracks with small tanks whizzing in and out, and a lot of yellow lines. To make matters worse, the parking meters have yellow bags over them which say 'NO PARKING NO LOADING NO WAITING'. Even stopping long enough to read the bags is an offence. You decide to risk it for a minute and run into the hall to find the man in charge. You ask him what the parking arrangements are.

'Your first time, is it?' he asks, a roll-your-own-fag skilfully grafted to his lower lip. You expect the fag to waggle while he talks but not only does it stay still, the inch of ash stays on as well.

'Yes, I'm on a yellow line at the moment.'

'Well you'll probably be OK.'

'But what about parking arrangements?'

'Arrangements?' He looks puzzled, but sympathetic. 'There aren't any actual, well not what you'd call *arrangements*. Not as such.'

'Well, what then?'

'If a warden's about, the exhibitors usually make sure everyone knows.'

'And?'

'Well, that's it really.'

By the time you return to your van, the street has filled with other

It is most unlikely that your exhibit will bear any
resemblance to your original plan.

exhibitors' vehicles from which are emerging trolleys laden with trees and shrubs. The small military tanks, driven by what look like little boys, but must be grown up soldiers, still weave about between them while a grizzled sergeant bawls instructions loud enough to be heard above the noise of the engines. Every other word he uses is a short Anglo-Saxon term for a basic biological function, which has startled some flower arranging ladies into dropping their materials in the middle of the street. Your van is boxed in by large lorries belonging to Hillier or Notcutt, so you decide to stay put and begin carting your stuff in.

Two things will dawn on you once you start staging your exhibit. First, creating a pretty stand will take much longer than you thought, and second, it seems everyone has had the same basic design idea as you. Sooner or later – usually a hell of a lot later – you are near enough completion to creep away, worn out, either to negotiate the traffic on a homeward drive or to your hotel, friend, club or whatever.

Next day the show will begin. Judging at ten thirty, public in at eleven. You arrive at the hall at nine, to give yourself time to put any little mishaps right and to do the finishing touches. Remember that lovely old oak branch you erected to give your display height? Well, at least it only fell on half the primroses. Lucky you've an hour and a half to put things right. At ten o'clock, when you are about half-way through your repairs, a bell rings and a man comes round to say exhibitors must leave. The schedule may say judging is at ten thirty but in reality it always begins at ten o'clock – another example of the RHS's gift for vagueness. You do a frantic last minute bodge and go to pace the streets, waiting miserably for the public to arrive. The public are usually let in before any of the exhibitors have got back to their stands, so you have to fight your way through a rising tide of humanity. You will then be on your feet – sitting is forbidden in the halls – for another nine hours.

Knowing the regulations is vitally important. Most people break a few, but you must know exactly where you are and how far you can go. Every plant must be clearly labelled, but don't try to be clever and label the logs or the moss. The judges lack anything approaching a sense of humour and are likely to downgrade you because your logs are dead, or because your moss is wrongly identified. A little gimmick can help – not with the judges, of course, but with the public. I always made sure a correctly labelled weed was included somewhere in my exhibits – a celandine perhaps, or a little groundsel plant. Once, when I had a nice specimen of great willowherb secreted among the tall stuff in the middle, I forgot to label it. I had sited it near a *Salix subopposita,* properly labelled, which has roughly similar leaves. The judges had a field day, thinking I'd confused the weed with the real willow. It was the only time any judge had every noticed my weed gimmick, but it cost me a good medal. People still ask me to remind them what the pretty willow with the uncharacteristic pink flowers is.

The whole exercise is unbelievably exhausting but has its lighter moments, especially when it's over. When showing, I usually stay at a certain club where jacket and tie are obligatory. Not being a native Londoner, I prefer to wear a suit in Town anyway, but filthy old trousers and a worn flannel shirt are more suitable for building up the stand. One of the pleasures at the end of staging day is to have a quick wash, don a suit and sink gratefully onto one of the bar stools at the club to indulge in drinks and chat. Imagine how silly I felt when, once, surrounded by immaculate city gents, I raised a neatly trousered leg and noticed I was still wearing filthy plimsolls with the toes poking through.

Foot-in-mouth opportunities abound at the London shows, especially if, like me, you have a penchant for saying the wrong thing to the wrong person at the wrong time. A distinguished-looking woman stood near my stand for quite a while during my fourth show. By then, about six months since my first exhibit, I felt the weight of experience heavy on my shoulders. I smiled and nodded at her.

'Nice little display,' she said.

'Glad you think so,' I said. 'Pity the judges don't agree with you. They only gave me a silver, ignorant twits! They don't know what they're looking at half the time.'

Her expression froze. 'Well, we liked the layout,' she said, 'but some of your plants are immature, that's why we downgraded you.'

Colborn withdraws, face crimson.

Another time, the mouth, as large and loud as ever, landed me in it good and proper. We were exhibiting a certain plant – nameless I'm afraid; I'm far too chicken to reveal the awful details – which, to my knowledge, was a new, unnamed colour form of a species. A very unassuming little man sidled up to me during the show and said: 'You might like to know that has an official name now; it's called "X".'

'Is it indeed?' I said. 'Well that's a bloody silly name for a start. It doesn't describe the plant at all. In fact it would be difficult to come up with a more misleading name.' I found out later that the little man was not only a very prominent figure in horticultural circles, but had named the plant himself. Gulp!

You will need to listen carefully to public reaction to your exhibit. After all, it is your public that really matters, whatever the judges have said about you. Remarks like 'takes me back to my childhood' and 'like a lovely wildflower meadow' are encouraging. You need to hear words like 'dainty' and 'old fashioned' as well as 'charming' or 'exquisite'. If you hear people say 'fussy' or 'out of character' or 'what a bloody mess!', you may have to improve your style a little. If someone says to you, 'What a display!', they're probably just trying to be polite.

Mind you, some very peculiar characters turn up at these shows. Once, when I was surrounded by customers six deep on all sides and revelling in all the attention, a sudden silence fell and, like greased lightning, everybody just de-materialised. A second or two later the most frightful smell welled up. As the last fan slipped away, I found myself looking at a gent of the road who obviously hadn't had a bath that morning or the one before or, indeed, since he'd walked away from the trenches in 1917. He turned out to be a fascinating character but it's not easy to hold a conversation and your breath at the same time. Eventually he left and I watched another crowded stand suddenly become deserted. One by one, people came back to our exhibit but several looked at their shoe soles carefully and then glared at me as if I'd been on a diet of beans.

Intense Questioners can be a bind too. The sort of person who is oblivious of the impatient queue behind, while they ask detailed questions about the culture of clematis, how to get sweet peas to germinate, or why they think euphorbias give them warts. A method of defence is the 'dive'. At shows, all your extra stock has to be stored under the staging so, when you want to bring out fresh plants, you have to do a reverse limbo dance, bending your body into a shape that will go under the 2-foot gap to reach for the flowers without crushing them. Most Intense Questioners take the hint if you say, 'Excuse me,' and get your head as far under the staging as you can. Of course, there are those who will continue the questioning, addressing themselves to your bottom with just as much intensity.

Proper Labelling

Nowhere is there more scope for animosity between rival experts than in the naming of plants. The RHS has a whole set of rules devoted to the subject. You have to put the genus and species names in italics, the cultivar name in single quotes and go through all sorts of other rigmaroles to comply. Most of the rules are hard to understand, some defy reason. Rule 6,c for new names reads as follows:

> Forms of address likely to be confused, e.g. "Mr." and "Miss", should be avoided unless national custom requires them (e.g., 'Ellen Willmott', not 'Miss Willmott' or 'Miss Ellen Willmott'); but "Madame", "Mrs" and equivalents in other languages are permissible.

People are always trying to alter the names of other peoples' plants:

'We're trying to decide what that iris *really* is,' says the 'expert'.

'It's what it says on the label, *Iris clarkeii*,' replies the exhibitor. This is greeted with politely scornful laughter.

'*Clarkeii*'s been out of cultivation for years. Sylvia Dado-Pannal is sure it's a *graminea* hybrid but I bet on it being just a form of *ruthenica*.'

'And your name is?'

'Cynthia Archetrave. I'm this year's chairperson of the Central Iris Group. Sylvia's president you know. You must have heard of her book.'

'I'm afraid not. I just grow the things.'

'But where did you get the plants from in the first place?'

'A packet of seeds.'

'I mean, where did the seeds come from?'

'The Central Iris Group. It was labelled *Iris clarkeii*.'

'Hmm. Can you remember the collector's initials on the packet?'

'It said "Collected S. D. hyphen P. 1988".'

There is no need to change the names of your plants if this kind of incident happens unless a TP corrects you. If that happens it is as well to comply with his wishes, even if you put a discreet question mark somewhere on the label, or the words 'thought to be'. The real problem arises when there are two or more TPs about, each one giving a specific plant different names. This happened to me once over a *Salix* which played a small rôle in one of my stands. It was a fairly good form of purple osier, *Salix purpurea,* with showy, wine-red stems and blue-green foliage. The two TPs, both female ran head on into each other in front of the offending willow.

'That's wrongly labelled,' said the first stridently, not, as I had thought, to me but over my head to a second woman coming up behind me. I didn't exist.

'Well, we both know that,' said TP number two, 'but is it *gracilis* or is it *pendula?*' I didn't realise at that time that both the plants they mentioned are forms of *S. purpurea* anyway. However, cowed as ever by TPs I though it best not to argue. They moved into a vigorous argument about how and why it couldn't be this or that willow. About how Imogen Sidecracker's was a prettier form anyway, about how the great Reginald Farrer had done such fine work on these small willows (which I don't think he had) and so on, all about a poor little British wild tree. Eventually I began trying to get a word in but it was no good; I still didn't exist. Finally, one of them said, 'We'll see what its pussies are like and then decide.'

'Golly!' I thought. 'What a strange woman.'

Then her opponent turned to me and said, 'When *does* it pussy up?' I was speechless. Finding out I existed after all was shock enough, but what a question!

My confidence was so shattered by these experts that I drove all the way to Westonbirt later that year to study the plants at the National Willow Collection. It was as I thought, just plain old *Salix purpurea,* except that, with willows, no two plants ever seem to be exactly alike. It goes to show, it's not what you know but how you say it! The expertise is just a cloak you put on.

A year or so of showing at Westminster and elsewhere will provide you with enough experience to handle Chelsea. But will you have the energy?

Chelsea

Chelsea is more than just a flower show. It is part of the British way of life. It begins the London season. This used to be the traditional starting date for the debutantes to 'come out'. These days Chelsea marks the beginning of the season when you can't get tickets for a play or an opera for another four months, when English is no longer spoken in central London and when important monuments like Big Ben, Nelson's Column and Goodge Street tube station are covered in scaffolding. Somebody in authority, a few years ago, found out that tourists were still photographing these edifices, in spite of the scaffolding, so they sent out a decree that all scaffolding was to be covered with a million opaque plastic sheets so that the whole monument was completely hidden. (Could this have been masterminded by the postcard industry?)

Exhibiting at Chelsea is quite an experience. You arrive with your van a day or two before the show begins. If you thought parking was difficult outside the halls, try doing it in the Hospital Grounds. Every available space is full of bits of conservatory, lawn mowers, garden seats and workmen eating sandwiches. Inside the great marquee – several acres of canvas – there are no vehicles but a sea of plants, pots, scaffolding poles, rope, wires and hundreds more workmen eating sandwiches. When you find your pitch, you realise, with a sinking feeling, that every single item will have to be carried 300 yards into the marquee.

From the exhibitor's point of view, the main difference between Chelsea and Vincent Square is that Chelsea runs for four days and you stand up for twelve hours a day, instead of nine. You also get to glimpse the royals. On the Monday, as midday passes, the chaos in the marquee begins to subside while the magnificence of the displays develops. Outside, the landscaped gardens are completed and various celebrities are being photographed with their faces buried in flowers, or in Chelsea pensioners, depending on their sex and their preferences. Rubbish is being cleared away, conservatory makers are making whoopee with the Windolene, and the press are here.

The press at Chelsea are a mixed blessing. Naturally, one wants a mention in as many organs as possible. At the same time, when panic is setting in and you think you'll never get done in time for the royals, the last thing you want is an in-depth discussion on the virtues of paeonies with a hack who probably knows more about the fighting in the Middle East than he does about plants and gardens. Naturally, the media gardeners are there in force. Some have polished their wigs for this occasion, others their heads. Television cameras lurch and sway in the aisles like science fiction monsters and you find yourself beaming into all of them – just in case!

Suddenly, at about four in the afternoon, the marquee is nearly empty. The pressmen are gone and the judges are hard at it. Each stand is surrounded in turn by the appropriate judging committee. A careful and thorough appraisal is made with lengthy discussion taking place. Judging a stand can take as long as fifteen seconds, but that is only for really large stands. The judges go to great lengths not to be caught judging stands that are being admired by the royals. This means that a game rather like a cross between tig and hide and seek takes place. A group of judges will make a little dash for a display on one side just as a prince or a duchess and their entourage are moving away from the other. The real hush falls in your area when the Queen arrives. Invariably, because they have done such a good job of avoiding the minor royals, the judges' committee doing your stand will arrive at exactly the point you hoped your hand might get a royal squeeze. Both parties waver and change course. The result? A poor award because nobody really looked at your exhibit and no chat with Her Majesty either.

Once the excitement of the royal visitors has subsided, the real work has to begin. Every member of the public who visits the Chelsea Flower Show deserves a medal for bravery. They begin pouring in at eight o'clock on the Tuesday morning, in silk skirts, elegant hats, polished shoes, neatly creased trousers. By ten, the hats have collapsed in the rain, the shoes are blackened in the mud and women who opted for open toes have black feet as well. Tuesday and Wednesday are laughingly called the 'private view' days because only members of the RHS can go. There are more than a hundred thousand of them. By midday it is impossible to see anything unless you are well above average height.

There are one-way systems in the marquee but only British visitors take any notice of these – evidently a large red disc with a white bar across only means 'no entry' in Britain. In theory, at Chelsea you should be able to talk to the nurseryman about the merits of his plants and give him an order, or even seek out a firm that has failed you and give the appropriate man a raspberry. In practice, you are moved bodily along with the tide of humanity. You can't stop, you certainly can't see many of the exhibits and the exhibitors are probably hiding under the staging or recovering from asphyxia in hospital.

Matters are worse outside. If you want to get to the lavatories you are in deep trouble, especially if you are in a hurry. It's worse for women; they have to queue up for ever, at busy times. For an exhibitor, this kind of delay can spell disaster. It can take half an hour or more simply to weave through the mass of people to get to the bogs and back again, by which time your partner on the stand may be prostrate.

By the end of the day, you will have pushed your body and mind well beyond the realistic limits of endurance. You'll have met so many important people and made so many vital contacts to further your career as a gardening expert that, although physically knackered, mentally you will be flying higher than Concorde. You are living on adrenalin and an occasional over-priced and disgusting sandwich on sale at the exhibitors' canteen. Come five o'clock and the sell-off begins. It coincides with your slide down into reality.

The first blow to your feeling of well-being comes when the bell rings and the crowds of vultures who have been waiting by your stand for half an hour start clawing it to pieces with their bare hands. Various plants are to go home with you, being too rare and special to sell. Others are booked by show visitors who will collect them later. But here you are in the midst of a display of human avarice at its worst. Hands appear from behind the front phalanx of buyers, grabbing plants and disappearing into the crowd. You feel yourself change from the benign personality, beaming at the customers, into a snarling tiger. '*Put that back!*' you scream at an innocent-looking little old lady who has just lifted your rarest plant into her bag. '*Get back!*' you shout at the thickest part of the crowd where people are actually climbing up onto your ruined stand. Then, feeling like a lion tamer, you grab plants, bag them, take the money and thrust them into the frantic hands of the mob. Heaven knows why they do it. Who, in their right mind, wants to buy a plant that has been forced for the show and then suffered almost a week in a hot tent? Do they think they're getting bargains?

Eventually they go. All that is, except the eccentrics who sift through the rubbish skips for fragile trophies like broken roses and browning lilies. You are left with the mess and the job of getting home. This is the point where the RHS management and men demonstrate their expertise. They manage, with minimum loss of temper and maximum efficiency, to get every vehicle on and off the premises that evening. You can hardly believe the speed with which the flower show degenerates back into a vast area of wreckage and finally an empty site, all rubbish cleared away and ready to give back to those patient and endearing old fellows in their snappy uniforms – the Chelsea Pensioners.

And when it's all over, what do you remember most? The exhibitor who threw a tantrum because his stand was 5 inches smaller all round than he ordered? The way you clapped what you though was an old friend on the back and said, 'Hello lovey, how the hell *are* you?' realising too late that it was Germaine Greer and though you may know her, she sure as hell doesn't know you! The man who got muddled and curtseyed to the Queen? Or the restful hour spent sitting in your van on King Albert Bridge, waiting for your turn to get into the ground while your partner slaved away packing everything up. The most vivid memory I have of Chelsea was driving home exhausted and starving, not having eaten properly for days, and stopping half-way up the A1 for a meal at dead of night. The only place open was a Chinese take-away whose food was so memorably foul that even in our famished state we were unable to eat it and had to complete the long journey home with all the windows open to get rid of the horrible smell.

Chapter 4

Coping with Judges

'A judge must take care to see that he is not swayed by his essentially personal views.'

(*The Horticultural Show Handbook* 1981,
Royal Horticultural Society)

In the palmy days of my youth – can it really be a quarter of a century ago? – I had the privilege of sitting next to Timothy Leary at dinner. 'Who the hell is Timothy Leary?' I hear you cry. Well, I'll tell you.

It was the sixties. Flower power was in, girls had given up skirts and were wearing thick cloth belts instead – nice fashion idea, shame about most of the girls' legs. Boys grew their hair to shoulder length and handed round daisies with remarks like 'Peace, brother', and 'Make love, not war', and occasionally even, 'Anyone here called Sergeant Pepper?' In the United States, where I studied for nearly half the sixties, our main preoccupations were Vietnam, civil rights and LSD – not necessarily in that order. One of the world's most prominent cult figures in those days, when we confused liberty with licence, was a discarded university professor who wanted hallucinogenic drugs like LSD to be legalised. Actually sitting next to such a famous bod caused me physically to shake. 'This guy is a living legend', I thought, 'he's had the guts to bring his philosophy, however unpopular with the establishment, out into the world and to live by his extraordinary credo'. I passed him the salt with a hand that quivered reverently.

Next morning, we bumped into each other again in the student union building.

'Did you eat breakfast yet?' he asked.

'No', I replied, 'I always have it after my eight o'clock lecture. Physical chemistry. I hate it.'

'You actually *go* to your eight o'clocks?' he asked, as if conscientiousness was a vice.

'Sure. Then I get breakfast.'

'Could I come along too?'

'By all means.'

'By all means!' he mimicked my accent, 'I love that. It's so . . . so . . .'

'Quaint? Shakespeare-ish?'

'No, more like the Beatles.'

'Thanks very much!'

We selected our breakfasts at the cafeteria – mine a good deal more modest than his – and when we got to the till, he began the most unconvincing struggle to find his wallet. Eventually, after a great deal of symbolic pocket tapping, he produced an expensive morocco affair and opened it. 'Look,' he said, 'empty.'

'Oh, no problem,' I said, and paid for both breakfasts. As we ate, I began to interpret this great permissive philosophy. In a nutshell it said: 'Why buy your own breakfast when the world is littered with suckers who'll pick up the bill?' Clearly, I'd made a gross error of judgement. Not the first and certainly not the last – but one that shook me to the core.

Judgement is at the root of our existence. We base a myriad daily decisions on our own judgement. How good we are at making the right decision depends on how skilled we are at judging. Official judging is quite different. Wherever a committee is appointed and awards presented, the criteria for judging change completely. Show judging is a way of life, a profession, a calling.

One of man's deepest tragedies throughout history has been rooted in his inability to entrust decision-making to the individual. Take a team of the most brilliant minds, each a genius in his own right, put them round a committee table and the policy that issues forth will have the soundness of a paper house built on the Goodwin Sands at low tide. Examples of wasted talent are all around us: look at the Common Agricultural Policy, the R101 airship, the Government Think Tank. It's the same with judges' panels. Each member may be a sound and gifted expert who, left to judge on his own or with no more than one colleague, will perform soundly. But put a group of them together and what do you get? Pure fruitcake!

Judging takes place at all manner of events. Flower shows burst at the seams with judges, but they also preside over garden competitions, best kept village awards, flower arranging events and children's contests. Tidy Britain Group arranges a huge national affair called Britain in Bloom. Any community can enter, from a hamlet of 50 souls to a city of three million. Judges for these functions are recruited in a variety of ways. Nepotism helps and the 'old boy network' is as important here as it is in politics. As a budding gardening expert, you will certainly come under the scrutiny of a committee of horticultural judges sooner or later. You will also, once your star has risen, be expected to contribute to the good of all by offering your profound wisdom, experience and expertise to a panel of judges yourself. When the calling comes, be ready!

The Anatomy of a Judge

There are hundreds of different kinds of judge but the great majority of them fall into one of several basic categories. The most common of these are listed below.

The **'Self-Important' judge.** Usually male and always loud, this type never just comes into a room – he makes an entrance. He will usually make sure everyone anywhere near him knows that he is on any number of national committees, will wear badges showing his office at flower shows and will always be quick to offer gratuitous advice. He'll adore lecturing, and will tell you all about his subject – such people are often well versed in a very narrow field and can therefore only give one basic lecture – and unless you are able to take avoiding action, he'll give you a private hearing. This is quite interesting the first couple of times, but by the fifteenth show this season his monologue on tissue culture is wearing a little thin.

Equally self-important, but in a far more subtle way, is the **'Intensely Fanatical'** judge. There seem to be more females than males of this species as a rule, but the syndrome is far from exclusive to women. The Intensely Fanatical is usually a very quietly spoken person who seethes inwardly. Her field will often

Equally self-important is the *Intensely Fanatical* judge.

be broader than most and her knowledge deep. Flowers and plants may be a pastime for you but to her they are intensely important and there must be absolutely *no jokes*. She will be armed to the teeth with rulebooks – a positive suitcase full of them, dating back to 1888. She will also carry a thick, important-looking notebook in which she will make copious notes in tiny handwriting. She it is who prolongs committee meetings so that each exhibit can be discussed fully. At the judges' lunch, she will eat next to nothing and drink only a little Perrier water, in order to keep her mind fresh and clear. 'Dedication' is her key word and heavens! is she ever dedicated!!

'True Plantsmen' abound on judges' panels. They are far more amusing than Intensely Fanaticals but usually know their stuff. Many of them over-indulge at lunch and find that this tends to impair their impartiality. Also, they usually know and like all the exhibitors, which can play havoc with their objectivity. On the commercial displays, the TP's attitude varies according to who is exhibiting. If one of their favourite plants is on display, the sky's the limit as far as awards are concerned. If they hate sweet peas and you're a sweet pea grower – bad luck!

The 'Silent Creeper' is possibly one of the most dangerous judges to come up against. Silent Creepers say nothing during the actual process of judging. They tag along, usually at the back, keeping silent and taking no notes. Nobody asks their opinion and, anyway, during judging the only voices you are likely to hear are those of the TPs and the Self Importants. However, when the voting starts, the Silent Creeper jerks into action, voting for the lowest possible award – or for no award at all.

Finally, and most tiresome, is the 'Knocker' or 'Boat Rocker'. Knockers are often embittered people in real life too. (I say 'real life' because when judging one is in a completely different world, cushioned from reality by the judiciary privileges bestowed for the day.) While the rest of the panel is trying to assess each exhibit, the Knocker is striking at the very roots of the system. 'These shows get more pathetic every year,' he moans. 'Dear God! Fancy putting up *that* variety for competition. How the hell are we expected to judge blooms like that in this light?' and so on. If judging is on a points system, the Knocker awards zero as a protest against the system. If the evaluation is subjective, he'll downgrade everything – everything, that is, until an exhibit turns up that is so appallingly bad the other judges want to disqualify it. To this he'll recommend full marks, just because it goes against the grain.

Putting these five types onto a panel will result in a consortium that lacks almost every required quality for satisfactory judging. Add a drunk, a visually handicapped person and a manic depressive and you have the makings of a first rate committee. You can imagine what an informal gathering of such a committee would sound like:

Drunk: I'm sure we could dishcush all this more 'ffectively in th' beer tent.

TP: Good idea, old fruit! and so say all of us – what say Enid?

Silent Creeper: . . .

Self-Important: Well, OK, but just a teeny one. I've got to keep my wits about me. I'm giving the talk tonight, after the Gala Dinner. I'll be putting forward the relative merits of micro-propagatio . . .

Drunk: C'mon, we'll have t'hurry. They close in less'n'hour.

Intensely Fanatical: But getting back to that display of primulas on the Higginbotham stand, I do think it very important that we downgrade them for wrong labelling as an example to the others. I mean spelling Garryarde without an 'e'. It really is inexcusable. We can't let inaccuracies like that creep in.

Knocker: The whole thing is sick. This is supposed to be a rhododendron show, who the hell wants to look at bloody primroses anyway?

TP: I say. Steady on, Old Bean. Ladies present and all that.

Knocker: So what! You can't have it both ways. If they want women's lib they'll have to put up with a bit of raunchy language. I mean we're all equal now, aren't we?

Drunk: Look. Can we 'ave a drink or can we not?

Intensely Fanatical: I mean I'm quite aware that Higginbotham has staged the finest display of primulas this hall's seen for about twenty-five years but the point is, this is their first show and they need to be taught a lesson. It's so careless of them, ruining their chances like that. I think it's a matter for the show committee. Perhaps a stiff letter is in order if they're thinking of exhibiting again.

TP: I say, Daphne. That's a bit hard isn't it? Just for one letter. We need new exhibitors badly, besides, it was me who persuaded Victor Higginbotham to have a go. I say we overlook it.

Self-Important: Well, there's no way they'd have won a Gold anyway.

TP: Why not?

Self-Important: This is their first show. It isn't done.

Knocker: Typical! I suppose you have to be a Freemason to get on the show committee too!

Self-Important: What's that about the show committee? I'm chairman this year. I can assure you, selection is gone into very carefully. We only appoint the best brains, you know.

Knocker: Anyway, what the hell's Daphne on about? Griping about bloody labelling again. Why can't you turn a blind eye? Everyone else breaks the rules.

Intensely Fanatical: I happen to think it's important.

Knocker: Fine. Report to the committee by all means, dear. They'll do sweet Fanny Adams about it anyway.

(*They walk all 10 yards to the beer tent.*)

Drunk: Now whash't goin' t'be, Peter?

Self-Important: Just a half of lager. I want to be . . .

Drunk: We know! Daphne? Same? Clarence?

TP: Just shandy. Bit early for me, Old Thing.

Drunk: Simon?

Knocker: Christ, haven't they got any Real Ale? Typical! It'll have to be lager then.

Drunk: Now, Enid. Can I tempt you?

Silent Creepy: Er, could I possibly have a, um, 'boilermaker'.

Everyone: A what?

Silent Creepy: It's a double scotch with a pint of bitter chaser.

The Rules of the Game

'Three-fourths of the prizes awarded at country shows are given for subjects which ought not to be encouraged, or for productions which it requires no talent to produce. The former does not advance the cottager or his interests one jot; the other cannot exalt his feeling, or improve his mind.'

(*Annals of Horticulture*, Houlston & Stoneman, 1846)

The first and most crucial rule for judging of any kind is to exclude even the faintest shred of humour from your activity. It's a serious business and your decision about whether Mr A's sweet peas are more perfect than Mr B's will cause joy in the heart of one and deep anguish in the other.

With competitive showing there is always a schedule. An exhibit is either according to schedule or it isn't, so a judge who is unfamilar with the schedule – and they vary from show to show – is a potential show wrecker.

Judges are guided by a certain amount of hard statistical measuring – length, width, number of petals, number of flowers on stem – that sort of thing. Details to guide them come in publications like the *The Horticultural Show Handbook* which lists meritorious and defective qualities for an astonishing range of exhibits. That, however, is more or less where the objective assessment comes to an end. The rest depends on gut feel, plumping and 'wing and prayer' techniques.

When it comes to 'non-competitive' exhibiting, it's all subjective. 'Non-competitive' doesn't mean that exhibitors don't compete with each other. Far from it. It just means that there are status awards but the exhibitors aren't ranked. By far the most important contributors to the major national flower shows are the commercial nurseries. These firms lay out stands and displays of all kinds of plant material. They may be instant shrubberies, alpine rock displays, ranks of freshly cut flowers or even exquisitely designed water gardens. These are the exhibits most of the public pay to see. Without them, few gardeners would bother to go to the shows, which would then collapse through lack of support. In spite of this, judging is often at its very worst with commercial exhibits. To assess commercial exhibits along currently accepted lines, it is essential that judges have a thorough knowledge of the unwritten rules.

For example, it is essential to know who the exhibitors are. Usually, awards are given according to the number of years a firm has supported the show, to the size and status of the firm and to its track record of medals. The degree of artistic merit or rarity of plants used has nothing whatever to do with the quality of medal awarded. Awards are also ranked according to the types of plant exhibited. Orchids and bonsai are the highest medal earners, closely followed by rhododendrons, camellias and other acid-soil shrubs but *not* heathers. Gentians fit in here too. Next down the line come irises. A really bad iris exhibit will often receive a higher award than an excellent herbaceous perennial display. Moving on downwards, bulbs come next, especially small species bulbs. After that, and we're getting down into the dross now, come alpines (except gentians), specialist herbaceous plants like sweet peas, chrysanthemums or dahlias and fruit trees. Finally, at the very bottom, come herbaceous perennials which are hardly rated, and then fuchsias and pelargoniums which are despised in genteel judging circles – except, of course, by fuchsia and pelargonium specialists. At most big flower shows, house plants get little more than a second glance from the judges – unless they've been imported from Holland or Belgium.

Finally, it is essential that exhibitors are kept in the dark about what the judges expect of them. When you exhibit, don't bother to ask why your stand only picked up a small silver or a bronze when your neighbour won a gold for fewer varieties on a bigger area. Each member of the judges' panel, if they speak to you at all, will give you a different reason for this kind of anomaly. But there, that's part of the fun of showing. Next time it might be your turn to throw together a 'potboiler' and be surprised with a good medal. The great thing is never to be disheartened; keep showing for at least a decade – your turn to win will come – and never exhibit fuchsias.

The Judges' Lunch

Judges do quite a lot for horticulture. They give freely of their time, turning up to judge shows and events all over the country. Many of them have their own careers to follow and even the retired ones are usually active, busy people – one or two even have good gardens. Most organisations connected with amateur horticulture claim to be short of money. Clearly, large fees are out of the question in most cases. However, small perks or large lunches often work wonders in tempting judges back for another stint next year.

The Chelsea Lunch, on the Monday of Chelsea week, is the supreme example of a good blow-out in the interests of improving excellence in horticulture. All the journalists go as well as the judges and, what with all those foreign visitors and the President and Council and all the other worthy guests, it's quite a shindig, I can tell you. Because some of the more prestigious firms throw drinks parties on their stands all day, many of the journalists are pretty well oiled before they get to the official luncheon. A few never quite manage to find the President's tent, hidden discreetly away as it is in those woods behind the Embankment. These poor souls are often found days later, like Babes in the Wood, fast asleep, covered with leaves and empty crisp packets. Others get arrested for trying to break into the wrong side of the nearby lavatory tent.

The lunch itself is done very 'naicely'. None of yer old plate in one hand, glass in the other and balance the Scotch eggs on top of your head. There's a proper waitress service, four courses and wine. For the loyal toast there's champagne and for the melba toast there's smoked salmon. There are speeches too, of course – you'd never expect to escape without one or two of those. They're mostly self-congratulatory – 'This is the best Chelsea so far this year', 'I'm pleased to report that we now have non-rhododendron exhibitors outnumbered eight to one' – that kind of thing. When the formalities are over and the hacks have checked that all the glasses and plates are well and truly empty, the staff move in and the judges move out to begin their job of assessing the show through a vinous haze which, during the process of the afternoon, quietly subsides into a sharp headache. Their serenity gradually becomes ruffled as the royals start strolling in. By that time, their afternoon crapula has reached its peak and that, combined with fear of putting a foot in it with a prince or a duke, causes near apoplexy. At this stage in your showing career, if you see a judge on the horizon your only hope is to scarper. If you are a judge, on the other hand, and find yourself in this situation – well, hard luck. No one forced you to have that fifth glass of wine did they?

Not-Flower-Show Judging

From time to time judges, because they are deemed fit to assess chrysanthemums or carrots, are invited to take charge of non-floral events. This can mean anything from the men's knobbly knee competition at the village fête to judging the Miss World Beauty Contest. Naturally, the same sort of rules apply – knowing who the competitors are, who won last time, the political implications and so on.

Bottled fruits used to be all the rage. Nowadays, when everything gets frozen, Kilner jars are almost a thing of the past. Luckily, produce show organisers don't concern themselves with the state of our deep freezes at home. Even the most organised and efficient housekeepers lose things in the freezer bottom. (You'd need a degree in archaeology to catalogue the various layers of icy relics in ours.) For instance, the only time you can find any frozen raspberries is when you have a clear-out to make room for the new crop. There you are, kitchen wall to wall with red streaks and blobs – well, you would try to get the swallow to fly out of the window again *before* you put the over-full basket down, wouldn't you? Looks like a murder scene. You have fifteen foil trays filled with raspberries garnished with aphids, hay seeds and an occasional dead bee, but the deep freeze is full. You start hauling stuff out. What do you find? Twelve breasts of lamb – funny how the legs and shoulders always go first. Hello, what's this? Rubbing at the frosted labels, your hands numb and aching in the cold, you read: 'Pheasant, shot David Nov '77', 'Peas 198–', 'Pork loin 1986', and, of course, 'Raspbs '86' and oh look, here's another 'Raspbs' '84'. I wonder if they're still all right? Might do for cooking. So, what do you do? When your garden is groaning with fresh, sun-kissed raspberries, you're making some horrid concoction to disguise the stale taste of four-year-old relics from the freezer to make room for this year's harvest. Makes you wonder whether the grasshopper wasn't right after all, and not the ant!

With bottled fruit, prizes were supposed to go to those whose offerings kept their natural colour and shape as far as was possible. Of course, the bottles that go to the show were one in a thousand. For every jar of Miss Flora Print's perfect, golden greengages exhibited at the Lower Buttock Rose Society's Autumn Produce Show, there were ten jars of brownish sludge with a dozen plumstones floating in the top at home. There were still others with ominous bulges in the lids.

With jams, it was about the same. At home, the family might

eat, and enjoy, jams that were so well boiled you could slice them into pieces with your knife. In milk puddings they could be stirred round for five minutes leaving wonderful spiral patterns of purple on the creamy background. Next time round, cook having over-compensated, the jams were so liquid they were almost drinkable and wouldn't keep. By October they smelt alcoholic and by Christmas the mould on top was so thick you couldn't get at the jam. But at the show – first prize to Mrs Freda Buxomb for her near-perfect strawberry jam – the strawberries in the jar magically arranged in neat layers.

Try to judge this kind of show and you are walking in a minefield. For a start, you have no expertise. You may have particular tastes – perhaps you prefer cakes to be a bit heavy or dislike meringues unless they are chewy – but you don't really know what you are looking at. Secondly, there are about six winners and about 50 losers. All 50 will be sticking pins into images of you and the six winners tonight. Thirdly, you are going to be advised, aided and abetted by a co-judge, Lady Wyde-Buoy, wife of the millionaire chairman of Effluent Byeproducts PLC, Sir Darryl Wyde-Buoy. She knows everybody and everything, is feared and loathed by half the villagers but worshipped and adored by the other half. You are not sure where your sympathies lie. You are met at the tent by the committee who say, 'Good afternoon' rather stiffly and then withdraw while you deliberate.

'Where shall we start?' you say. 'This isn't really my line. I'm more a sweet pea and rose man.'

'Fruit cakes,' says your co-judge. You're not sure whether she means the committee or the exhibits. 'That's sad,' she continues.

'Well, I suppose it's difficult to find anyone else who'll serve on these little committees.'

'What *are* you talking about? I mean that fruit cake is sad.'

'Why? Has it lost its Mummy?'

'It's sunk in the middle.'

'Oh. I thought they did that on purpose so they could dollop more icing on.' You move on to the home-made wines. 'Aha!' you say, 'This is more my line.'

'So I've heard,' says your co-judge. You're beginning to know which side of the village you belong to – and it isn't the 'worship and adore' tendency. The first bottle is labelled 'Parsnip and Whortleberry' and contains a pink, cloudy liquid. You uncork, pour and sniff. No bouquet. You sip. Your mouth forms an involuntary rictus as the acid assaults your palate. You won't be able to speak for a few seconds so you watch for her reaction.

'What a charming label,' she says. 'Beautifully designed. Really quite artistic. It must be one of Rene Toogood's wines, she's such a dear soul.' She sips, not a flicker.

'Very palatable,' she says. 'It'll take some beating. Who's next?' She lifts a bottle of urine-coloured liquid marked 'Potato Peelings and Groundsel'. You both taste. It's not good but it's infinitely better than the Parsnip and Whortleberry. It tastes a bit like a very thin Riesling. You say so.

'Rubbish! Not a bit like Riceling – it's more like Mason. A very bad Mason.'

'Mason?'

'White burgundy. You're evidently not a wine expert.'

'Oh, Mâcon.'

'Mason. You're not much of a linguist either, are you? Let's get on.'

You try another amber liquid labelled 'Sylvaner type'. It's really not too bad. You'd almost be able to serve it to your guests, provided they were already reasonably tight. At least it's been made with grapes.

'This isn't bad,' you venture. 'In fact it's the best we've tasted so far.'

'Are you serious?' she looks scandalised. 'This is from that . . . that unnatural couple. Up on the down.'

'Unnatural? Oh, you must mean the Poofter Pooles. I think they're great fun. Yes, you're right, I believe they do have a few grape vines.'

'It ought to be illegal. It's disgusting. And dangerous.'

'Dangerous? Vine growing?'

'You know very well what I mean. Besides, it's against the laws of nature.'

'I thought we were judging home-made wine.'

'So we are. I'm for Rene Toogood. I thought her Parsnip and Whortleberry easily the best. I'm sure you'll agree.'

'Well, I . . .'

'After all. You said you were a sweet pea and rose man.'

'I suppose her labels were the prettiest.'

'Precisely.'

Later in the day, the results start rolling in. It comes as no surprise that most of the awards are shared between three people. Rene Toogood got twelve and the Print sisters, Flora and Liberty went home with nearly all the rest.

Beautiful Bloomers

These days, since we no longer manufacture anything in Britain, tourism has become one of our most important industries. The Tourist Boards use lots of our taxes on expensive public relations to entice foreigners to come to Britain, spend vast quantities of money and then go home taking fond and happy memories with them. Naturally, the big draws like York Minster, Stratford on Avon and Wigan Pier are already deeply committed to the tourist racket. Many other towns, cities and villages may not be prime attractions but, nevertheless, can do a great deal to tart up their surroundings. It is alleged that we are a nation of gardeners, so beautifying our towns and cities with colourful planting is likely to entrench the foreigners more firmly in their prejudice about us. This is seen to be good for business.

Every year, about a thousand communities, ranging from huge cities to tiny villages, enter the Britain in Bloom competition. Winners are selected in England, the Isle of Man, Northern Ireland, Scotland and Wales. After the heats, the national judges have a gruelling itinerary covering the whole nation in ten days to judge the finalists. The cities and towns spend extraordinary amounts of money on planting and gardening. Aberdeen, for example, buys 100 tonnes of daffodil bulbs every year. That's about six giant lorry loads! In Duthie Park there is a small hill planted with no less than 96,000 roses. Vast armies of gardeners maintain the city parks and gardens.

The cities and towns also spend quite a bit on the judges. This is in no way bribery or corruption, you understand, just an effort to make them feel welcome. Elaborate flowers and bowls of tasty fruit appear in their hotel bedrooms. Little souvenir bottles of single malt whisky, expensive coffee table books and whole libraries of glossy brochures help to triple the weight of their suitcases.

It's different for the village judges. They are not looking at vast corporation efforts resulting from spending mind-boggling amounts on nursery stock. In the villages, community spirit is the essential ingredient, but emotional blackmail is even stronger.

'We thought you'd like to have a cup of tea with Mr and Mrs Paraquotte. They're local farmers. The Paraquotte boys made all the brackets for the hanging baskets in their spare time.'

'Thank you. That would be lovely.'

'And this is Mrs Tittlethwaite's front garden. She's a widow, eighty-seven. Isn't she wonderful? And over here is a bedding display done by one-parent families. Oh yes, our vicar got all the children to do a competition and this is the result. A lovely display of flowers all round the church.' And so it goes on; every floral achievement was the result of a heart-rending effort by some unfortunate individual or other. Harmony reigns in the village for the duration of the judges' visit. Eventually, after walking the streets with an entourage of parish councillors, flower committee members and other camp followers, one is shepherded into a farmhouse for the aforementioned cup of tea. At the door there is a muted scuffle and whispered debate as the camp followers are separated from the official tea guests and ejected.

In the Paraquotte sitting room is a spread like a children's party. There are scones, bread and butter, flapjacks, shortbreads, fairy cakes, rock cakes, sponge cakes, fruit cakes, scotch pancakes, biscuits and chocolate fingers. Since the judges have had a substantial lunch and have another village to judge in an hour's time, this feast makes them groan inwardly while they say: 'How simply lovely! What a splendid tea! You *have* been busy!' and so on. Then the blackmail continues. Eyes bore into the back of your neck while the committee wait to see which cakes you'll accept and which you refuse.

'Do have one of these scones. Mrs Tittlethwaite'll be so thrilled if you like them.'

'You must try this sponge. Mrs Paraquotte's daughter has just been doing domestic science at school.'

'You're not making much headway with those rock cakes. Have another.'

Eventually, the goodbyes are said and you leap aboard your aircraft for the next place. It's a bumpy ride – it always is in light 'planes – and you feel just a thought queasy by the time you have landed and stepped out of the aircraft straight into the bosom of the next committee.

'Before you start judging,' says the chairman, 'the ladies have organised a little tea for you in the village hall. They do hope you'll accept.'

'How absolutely delightful,' you enthuse, 'Nothing we'd like better. We're starving and simply dying of thirst.' You walk into the village hall after being photographed for the *Lower Carnage Weekly Advertiser* and the *Rotten Sodbury Gazette*. Tables in the village hall are groaning under the weight of an even bigger tea which includes bowls of strawberries, clotted cream and several pork pies as well as everything you've already nibbled at in the last village. It's disconcerting to see that places have been laid. Everyone is to sit down to make a proper meal of it. Graciously, your hosts pile your plate with pork pie, ham sandwiches and pieces of fruit cake. When the time comes, you are not sure whether you'll be able to stand up. At this point the committee chairman says: 'We must get started. By the way, there are some very steep hills in this village. I hope you're feeling energetic because it's a tidy walk if we're to see everything.' The only thing that makes you force yourself to walk is the knowledge that in less than three hours you will be expected to sit down to a civic dinner with the mayor, the director of parks and gardens and about 50 other officials in the county capital. You need to work off a dozen cakes and six cups of tea. Judging has its perks, you see.

Of course, while you are developing your career as a garden expert, it is far more likely that you will spend at least the next few years on the receiving end of the process of judging. You will be the one exhibiting. Even if you don't want to go in for any show competitions – and many of our greatest experts never have – you are still likely to stage a stand or display, either as part of a society or with a commercial exhibit. Be ready for anything. *The Horticultural Show Handbook* says, in suggestion 14 on page 35:

Be a Sportsman. The judges' decision, whatever it may be, should be accepted with good grace. An exhibitor who has failed to get a prize and cannot at once see why, should search calmly and patiently for the cause of his competitors' success so that he, himself, may be successful another time.

This advice may seem to be self-contradictory. After all, a sportsman is someone who queries linesmen, disputes umpires' decisions and is rude and sullen with the press. Since top sportsmen frequently lose their tempers, it should be quite correct for horticulturists to do the same. But they don't. They take their judges' decisions with stoical self-control. Then, in the privacy of the pub or the local snack bar, they let rip.

'Need bloody white sticks.'

'I beg your pardon.'

'Judges. Like the blind leading the bloomin' blind.'

'You got a rotten medal then?'

'Didn't get one at all. Bastards!'

'Good Lord. That's practically a death sentence. What are you showing?'

'Begonias, coleus and African violets.'

'Oh well. That probably explains it!'

'What's wrong with 'em?'

'Well, they're . . . they're not quite the thing, are they? Judges aren't very enthusiastic about them.'

'What do you know about it? Yer first show innit?'

'First time I've exhibited. But I've been coming up here for thirty years. I can tell you, old boy, they don't rate your kind of plant.'

'But I grow them for a living. It's what I do. You know, me livelihood.'

'Nothing to do with it. If you want a medal you'll have to show something posh as well. Can't you borrow a few gentians or something? I could let you have some of my primulas if you liked.'

'Why, what medal d'you get?'

'Silver-gilt. I'd have got a gold only some silly old bag said one of my plants was wrongly labelled. Said I'd got the spelling wrong – so Fred told me.'

''Ow'd Fred know? 'E was supposed to be out of the tent durin' judgin', same as the rest of us.'

'Hid under his stand.'

'Get away!'

'Quite true. He was just crawling underneath to make sure his flask of gin was there ready for the show, when the bell went for exhibitors to clear out. He decided to stay under and listen in.'

'What, stayed there all the time? Bent double?'

'No. Just when the judges were finishing his stand he got cramp in his instep. He jerked up and banged his head on the side of the stand. Well, he had to crawl out then and slink off.'

'Who was this silly cow you was on about?'

'Daphne Mylton-Kienes.'

'Oh her! Mind you, she knows 'er stuff. She's about the only one who's ever talked to me. About African violets, I mean. Says I ought to have the original wild species on display as well as the cultivars. Dead keen, that's what old Daffers is. It's that other dame I can't stomach. Ena is it? or Enid? Yes, Enid.'

'Enid Skinfolk? The little quiet one, always hangs back. She wouldn't hurt a fly.'

'Don't you Adam and Eve it, mate. She may not say much but she don't 'arf know how to put the boot in on the markin'.'

'I thought she was a rather pathetic little creature. So meek and mild.'

'Gertcher. 'Armless as a rattlesnake. It's them meek and mild ones yer've gotta watch.'

It all seems rather cruel to say such horrible things about good-hearted folk who are only doing their best, but when you've done your share of exhibiting you'll soon discover a venomous streak you didn't know you had. If you ever hide under your stand, be prepared to hear some pretty damning remarks: 'Lovely camellias but he's such a horrid little man', or, 'There's not much point in any of us wasting time on this stand since we all hate fuchsias.'

So, you're now expert enough to be a judge and to withstand the onslaughts of judges yourself. My goodness, you are coming on well, aren't you? Here are a few more useful exercises.

1 Get some cards printed that say FIRST PRIZE. SECOND PRIZE and so on. Go off to your local greengrocer and begin judging the produce. Remember to tick the proprietor off if you think any of his vegetables are not according to schedule. If you think he has done a particularly good job, tell him so. He will appreciate you praising him.

2 Go to as many small shows as you can and try to get among the exhibits before judging. Be sure to examine them closely – don't be afraid to handle them – and try to find out why they are likely to win or not to win. Slice an apple or two in half to get a good look at the pips; take a few petals off the roses to see how firmly they are attached.

3 During judging, wade in and interrogate the judges. Ask them why they are selecting certain exhibits and to tell you why they are ignoring others. Be sure, also, to find out what they had for lunch.

Chapter 5

Nursery Catalogues

'In good garden soil all these plants will flourish like weeds.'

(From *Unusual Plants,* Beth Chatto's catalogue)

AMAZING Bar-B-Q OFFER! screamed the headline in one of those glossy magazines – all adverts and designer page numbers. Pictured under the hyperbolic blurb was an object that looked like a cross between Concorde and a pram. There were wheels, spit roasting tackle, bellows and a set of utensils that would have done nicely for a spot of medieval torture – all for less than £30. It looked big enough to roast a whole ox and sturdy enough to have withstood Napoleon's Russian campaign. We sent for it.

Eight weeks later, as the first autumn gales were getting started, a small flattish parcel arrived. Inside were various pieces of bent metal and a packet of screws. After about twenty hours, which included careful study of the instructions – something was lost in the translation from Serbo-Croat we felt – during which I skinned a couple of knuckles and blackened a thumbnail, we had assembled a flimsy toy just about big enough to roast a whole quail. On its trial run, a wheel fell off and hot ash spread all over the lawn. Second time out, the charcoal burnt through the pan at the bottom. End of amazing Bar-B-Q. Buying by post can be something of a lottery. Evidently, it would have been better to have gone to the local garden centre for our barbeque – at least we'd have had a chance to examine the goods before making our choice.

Though splendid for gnomes, barbeques and Christmas tinsel, the maddening thing about garden centres is that they are such disappointing sources of interesting plants. They're fine for bedding and common shrubs, but few stock anything very unusual. For these special treasures you need specialist nurseries. No serious gardener can afford not to deal with such nurseries for each one is an Aladdin's cave of treasures. The pain about most of them is that they are miles from anywhere and therefore can only be dealt with regularly by post – back to the lottery again!

Some of these nurseries are famous. They may be attached to great gardens or associated with an established and popular personality. Plants from such places have high status value and your image as a garden expert will be enhanced by having them in your garden. Make sure you leave the labels on and swipe some extras to tie on purchases you may have made at less prestigious establishments. Posh plantmanship is all important and many quite ordinary and even ugly species are grown widely by the horticultural *cognoscenti* because a top garden hack may have mentioned he has a soft spot for them, or a famous landscaper might have used them in one of her colour schemes. It is also very important, when you are showing visistors round your garden, to be able to provide a little history of the plants in which you take a special pride. Naturally, you won't go dropping the source's full name all in one go, but will let little gems of conceit trickle out as you browse in the shrubbery: 'That's *Lathyrus aureus,* from Vita's of course, doesn't it look well with Bob's special daphne?' Your visitor will be taking the bait by now.

'Bob?'

'Bob McDendron.'

'What, *the* McDendron? Sir Robert?'

'Such a *fun* family, don't you think. Oh but how stupid of me, it was the other daphne that came from him. This one's from the physicist – you know, gardens in Devon, Berkland Snapper.'

'I don't know anyone called Berkland Snapper.'

'That's the place, silly. Not far from Plymouth.'

'Oh, you don't mean Manfred Schlickmeister?'

'Good God no! *Ghastly* little man. Wanted to get on the committee in our Daphne Group. Blooming cheek, just because he's collected all those wild species in Asia. Thinks he's an authority or something. No not him. Similar name . . . Oh, dear me what *is* his name . . . something anatomical . . .'

'Foot? Hand?'

'Dicks! Lord Dicks. Chairman of the World Council of Physical Researchers.'

'But he lives in Geneva.'

'I know, but he spends his weekends at Berkland Snapper.'

'And they sell plants?'

'Of course. Their head gardener has a splendid little nursery. You should go. Why not pop over next weekend?'

'We can't. We're staying with friends down in Sussex.' (Your visitor will be fighting back by now.)

'Oh really. Anywhere nice?'

'Place near Northiam. Wonderfully ancient house. Redone by Lutyens.'

'Really. Anyone I know?'

'Up to a point.'

'Good garden?'

'Definitely.'

Mail order nurseries can be very efficient and helpful. They can also be a nightmare. If you have started producing plants to sell, you will find out very quickly that customers also fall into one of those two categories. The first step to a good mail order service is to have a well written and enticing catalogue. You can worry about whether you've got the plants later. Indeed, there are some nurseries that make as much income from catalogues as from plant sales. This is especially useful at flower shows like Chelsea where selling plants is forbidden until the end. A decent catalogue might sell 3,000 or more copies at £1.00 each. Add to that the proceeds from 1,500 packets of seed at £1.00 each and you have a tidy sum – as you find out when, at the end of the show, you've got about 90 kilos of coinage to lug home. Some catalogues become valuable handbooks, serving as reference works long after they have gone out of date, sometimes even after the nursery in question has ceased to exist. A few nurserymen have gone as far as to 'publish' them, usually under a pretentious title and in hard cover as a *'Dictionary' of* . . . or an *'Encyclopaedia' of* . . .

Downmarket firms resort to brilliant colour illustrations and a jazzy image. Others use their literary skills to full advantage, producing little classics that throw the best garden writers into shadow. Plant descriptions haven't quite got to the ludicrous extremes of newspaper wine correspondents yet – well, at least not the kind of prose you find in the 'quality' papers:

Touraine de la Pseud du Tout: cheeky little quaffing wine with the familiar gooseberry flavour of the Loire augmented with a hint of blackcurrant, beech leaves and dustbin bottoms. Not too much body, light and fruity, sixth, out of the ten we tasted.

You're not sure whether the last bit refers to the wine or the taster. Nursery writers fall short of that kind of language but, each year, certain descriptions grow more wordy. Just before we stopped selling plants by mail order, a man rang to ask why he hadn't received our latest catalogue.

'There isn't one,' I told him. 'You can only buy plants if you come to see the gardens.'

'Good God, I don't want to buy any plants,' he replied. 'They're far too expensive. I just enjoy reading your catalogue. It's a guinea a minute.'

'Pity it doesn't earn me that much,' I muttered, my knuckles whitening on the 'phone.'

'What?'

'Perhaps you'd prefer something cheap and Dutch,' I amended. 'Try the van der Ripthof Bulb Co.'

'Oh thank you. I'll get onto them. Entertaining, are they?'

All mail order catalogues are prone to exaggeration and inaccuracy. Some verge on the criminal, others just paint the lily a bit. (Yes it is 'paint', not 'gild'; if you want to be a truly *pedantic* plant expert you must get little details like this right.) For brazen lies certain glossy bulb catalogues take the biscuit. (The catalogues are glossy, not the bulbs, silly.) They're not too bad on the big, vulgar hyacinths and tulips but in the sections on small bulbs they take the Hollywood treatment too far. Cyclamen give them the most trouble. It seems inconceivable to some merchants that people actually *like* their hardy cyclamen to have small flowers. Instead of showing a good picture of *Cyclamen hederifolium*, the most popular autumn-flowering species, they insist on calling it *Cyclamen neapolitanum* and illustrate a big indoor cyclamen thrust pot-first into a heap of peat. *Cyclamen repandum*, a common European native which is a bit of a swine to grow in English gardens, they call *Cyclamen europaeum*. But *C. europaeum* is actually the outdated name of a very rare plant now called *C. purpurascens* which only grows wild in parts of Europe. Occasionally they get these names right, but never the pictures.

Another mean trick they play is to misrepresent colour and size. A number of quite reputable firms illustrate one species or variety with another, more showy version. There are even cases of unrelated plants being shown. For example, a popular nursery based in southern England uses a well-coloured *Lunaria rediviva* to illustrate the choice, but less photogenic *Mertensia ciliata*. Isn't it ironic that the *Lunaria's* colloquial name is perennial honesty! As for changing colours, everyone knows there is no such thing as a blue rose or a blue gladiolus. Hybrid teas like 'Blue Moon' and 'Sterling Silver' are dirty lavender grey, but flick through certain catalogues and you will see a sapphire-blue flower with the words UNIQUE or NOVELTY flashed across it. 'Heavens', you think, 'they really have bred a blue rose at last.' Don't you believe it! Besides, who wants a blue rose? The idea is as repulsive as a pink delphinium, a yellow hellebore or a green daffodil – what? There is? Well, whadyaknow!

Worse than any inaccuracy and more heinous than any exaggeration is the mail order nursery that substitutes without permission. The whole point, these days, in buying by post is that it enables you to deal with distant firms who produce plants that nobody sells locally. How infuriating it is therefore, when you order a rare old pink, for example, like 'Brympton Red' and they send you 'Doris' which you could have bought at a fifth of the price in your local market. This practice is enough to drive the most patient soul wild. If you went to a shop and asked for black treacle you'd be pretty narked if they fobbed you off with golden syrup. If you ordered a Ford and they delivered a Vauxhall or vice versa, you'd be vexed. So why is it considered fair enough to substitute in the plant trade?

Going to flower shows, looking at other people's gardens and reading your gardening books will give you a fairly clear idea of what you want for your new planting schemes. Armed with a pencil and a calculator, you set about your accumulated pile of catalogues with a vengeance. The first step is to draw up a list of everything you want. You tot up the cost and, when you have regained your composure, you run through the whole thing again culling about two-thirds of the plants. Finally, you send off your revised order, prepaid as requested with a cheque and settle back to wait for the exciting task of unpacking your goodies. Since the firm 'regret that, owing to rising costs, they no longer acknowledge orders', you have no clue whether they have received yours, or when the plants will arrive. Eventually, the whole event sinks into the distant haze of your memory.

Months later, two days before you leave for a three-week pony trekking tour in the Dordogne, a postcard comes to inform you that your 'esteemed' order was despatched by Tortoiseline Freight that morning. It arrives on the day your ferry sails for Calais. But what's this? You expected at least three large boxes. 'Is that it?' you ask the driver.

'Yus mate. Sign 'ere,' he says, cramming a clipboard under your chin and a ballpoint pen up your nose.

'But it says "received in good condition". Shouldn't I open the parcel first?'

'Leave it art, mate, I've got forty free more drops yet. Then I've got ter git darn ter Fort Neef befower noine ternoight.'

'Fort Neef. Isn't that in Scotland?'

'Nar. London mate, you know, Fornton Heaf. Nar, are yer goin' ter sign or what?'

You sign. The lorry goes. You open your parcel. Inside are twenty of the 93 plants you ordered. Also inside is a copy of your order with some remarks scribbled on every entry. Thirty of the plants are 'to follow, spring'. Twenty-seven are 'regret unavailable'. Fourteen have been substituted because you didn't notice the tiny print at the bottom which said if you didn't instruct them otherwise they'd substitute with something similar. (Trying to work out what similarities exist between aubrietia and mountain ash will be a nice little brain teaser for you while you're on holiday.) Two plants are marked 'not grown at this nursery'.

You pick up the plants that have come out of their newspaper cocoons. 'That's funny,' you think, 'I thought I asked for five *Smilacina racemosa*. They've only sent one small one.' Then you unwrap the inner layer of packing which says 'Smilaxne rasse-mowsa X 5' and the plant falls into five tiny fragments. Your planting plan goes to the wall and you spend a frantic twenty minutes shoving your tiny withered purchases into the ground wherever there is space so that you can get off to France and forget the whole damn business. Try another nursery next time. It might be different.

As a budding gardening expert, you may be planning to create your own mail order nursery. If you do, you'll soon find out that the obverse of the coin can be just as nasty. Most customers are absolute darlings, but there are those who are a touch short of perfect. These come in several categories, but every aspect of your trading with them is made more difficult because the dialogue is by correspondence. The worst thing about a letter is that you can't unsend it. When it drops beyond your reach into the pillar box you've had it, even if you cool off and regret writing. Receiving nasty letters is nearly as unsettling. They always arrive during breakfast and you know it will be hours or even days before you can do anything about it. Staff at the Inland Revenue know this and always time their nastiest demands to arrive on the Saturday morning of a bank holiday weekend, or on Christmas Eve when you know there is no chance of getting hold of your accountant before the festivities are over. It's part of a softening-up process.

Everyone copes with difficult letters in his own way, but common to all of them is the fact that there is never a straightforward solution:

'Dear Sir, the Campanulas you sent me are all dead, I demand a refund.' . . . No problem there. A straight fact, simple action required: replace the plants free of charge if you think it was your fault. Offer sympathy, but nothing more if you think it was theirs. Either way, they are unlikely to buy from you again. What about:

'Dear Sir, I was quite pleased, on the whole, with your last consignment of plants but was most put out by your use of newspaper to wrap them in. The plants wrapped in *The Times* caused no offence but I think you ought to know that my mother, who is eight-five, was quite shocked when she found that others had been wrapped in *The Sun*. Please make sure all future orders are wrapped in plain paper . . .' Surprising, this. It confirmed my suspicions about our new packer because his predecessor used to save all the page three pictures. I suppose I ought to have smelt a rat when he pinned up photographs of Michelangelo's *David* in the potting shed next to the medal cards.

'Dear Sir, the plants you sent last autumn were received in good condition. Unfortunately, after the hardest winter we have ever experienced, most of them have died and we will need replacements or our money back. Please see to this matter at once.' This is clear cut. The plants are dead. It's not your fault. Compensate him and you've admitted responsibility for the winter. Refuse him and you've made an enemy for life.

Once a man accused us of tricking him into having plants he didn't order: 'Dear Sirs. I received a parcel of plants from you today. I did not order them and will not pay for them.'

We replied: 'Dear Mr X, Thank you for your letter. I'm sorry you no longer want the plants. We enclose a photocopy of your original order which appears to be in your handwriting and bears your signature. Our account is enclosed for your attention.' He paid in full but enclosed an unprintable letter with his cheque. He also swore we'd get a special guest appearance on Esther Rantzen's *That's Life,* but it was an empty promise – worse luck!

Faint praise can be very demoralising. There's not much you can do about it other than take it on the chin. In many ways abuse is easier to accommodate:

'Dear Sirs, Your consignment of penstemons arrived here this morning after two weeks in the post. I expect they will survive but reserve the right to claim from you if they do not. They are quite nice plants but a little too forward for late dispatch. Plastic wrapping would have been more suitable than newspaper and a typed address might have found us more quickly. No doubt you are still finding your feet . . .'

Some customers are terrible mind changers. This is bad enough over the counter, but by post it can cost a small fortune. Inevitably, there will be a mix-up because you didn't add the latest additions or subtract the latest removals. Sometimes the alteration comes too late and the customer ends up with the wrong things altogether. You are never quite sure who is in the wrong in these circumstances but, naturally, the customer is always right, and will write to put you right.

Dealing with hundreds of customers, some mistakes are inevitable. However hard you try, these will all be made with the same customer so even though you are a useful and efficient outfit to most people, to certain folk you are a disorganised rabble:

'Dear Sirs, I'm writing to tell you that I shall no longer be buying plants from you. My nerves won't stand up to the strain. I asked for oxlips. You sent cowslips. I complained. You sent plants labelled "oxlips" within a couple of days. When they flowered, they turned out to be cowslips anyway. You apologised and promised to find a more reliable source.

'Last week I received a parcel from Pritibig Plant Supplies PLC. The invoice said "to supplying six *Primula elatior* (Oxlips) £5.40, charge to Colborn." Underneath, somebody had crossed this out and written "Oxlips sold out. Substitute Cowslip". Since my paddock is full of cowslips, I gave these plants to my friend in Higher Morgidge but when they flowered they turned out to be oxlips. She was not very happy because, though her woodland garden is full of oxlips, she has been trying to get hold of some cowslips which are rare in her part of the world. She thinks she is forbidden from digging any of her oxlips up for me because they are protected by law.

'What am I to do? My doctor has suggested I take up dog breeding. Yours truly. Edith Weston, Ms.'

Correct Interpretation

The most important aspect of dealing with any plant catalogue is being able to understand and interpret the meaning of the language. The highly pictorial pamphlets are easy to handle. If you've read this chapter carefully you'll know by now that the pictures are all inaccurate with gross exaggerations of colour, size and so on. The producers will have gone to extremes to do this. They will look for a specimen plant to photograph and fix lots of extra flowers to it. They'll stand on their heads to get good camera angles and frequently print the photograph upside down. All is sham. It's all rather like the picture of the ravishing model you see in fashion magazines wearing her £6,000 *haute couture* dress. She looks wonderful from the front of the page but the reason her lips are pursed in that pensive way is not because she's thinking alluring thoughts but because she's got 51 clothes pegs holding everything together at the back. One false move and she falls apart.

In these cheap and bright catalogues there are words that spell danger. 'Novelty,' for example, means 'rather ugly, but might appeal to the cranks'. Such things as double columbines and orange arums are 'novelties'. 'New' means new to that particular firm. The plant may have been in cultivation for a hundred years. 'F1 hybrid' is usually confined to seed catalogues. It means the product is priced per seed rather than per packet. F1 hybrid vegetables usually yield twice as much as ordinary varieties, which does at least go some way towards making up for the astronomical seed price. Provided, that is, you get no pests like aphids, rabbits or caterpillars. They all prefer the taste of F1 hybrids.

Vegetable seed catalogues have their own special terminology. If, on any variety, it doesn't say 'high yielding' or 'heavy cropper', you must assume it is a low yielder. 'Delicate' or 'subtle' flavour means tasteless. 'Tender' means stringy, 'firm flesh' means stringy and 'traditional texture' means very stringy. In lettuces 'crisp' means limp and 'weather resistant' means stringy. 'Striking flavour' means 'tastes revolting'. 'Ideal for exhibition' means 'inedible but looks impressive'. 'Sweet Florence' is not the seedsman's daughter but a form of fennel.

'Rape' in vegetable seed catalogues is nothing whatever to do with Sweet Florence but a sort of brassica producing bitter leaves in winter. Don't confuse this with oilseed rape – those huge yellow fields seen everywhere these days. That is a farm crop invented by the European Community. The oil from rapeseed is mildly poisonous and the seed residue unfit for most farm animals. It also costs a lot more to produce than American soya (which has wholesome oil with a highly nourishing seed residue), so nobody wants it – a perfect EEC crop, in fact, and one which the Commissioners at Brussels thought would make the landscape look pretty. They used our taxes to pay farmers a lot of money to grow it, but somewhere between Rome and the Alps there is a lovely oil lake where holidaymakers can swim without fear of sunburn. It gives new meaning to the term 'slip into something loose', not to mention 'frying tonite'.

Correct interpretation is especially important when you are reading serious plant nursery catalogues. Unlike the glossy offerings that fall unsolicited through your letter box, these catalogues almost always cost money. They will be written by the nursery proprietor or someone in the family who fancies himself (or herself) as a writer. For literary merit, some of these works are pitched about half-way between Jane Austen and Christopher

Lloyd – that is, way above lesser men of letters like Flaubert, Keates and Wilbur Smith. Few see humour as an essential element, but there are exceptions and these sparkle like broken gin bottles on a sandy beach. As with vegetable seed lists, you must have a grip on the jargon. To help you with this, a series of translations follows.

'Needs a sheltered spot' – like a greenhouse in Torquay.

'Slow to increase' – It will still fit in the pot you bought it in after ten years.

'Grows best in full sun' – like in Tangiers.

'Graceful' – falls over.

'Arching stems' – doesn't fall right over but tends to collapse under its own weight, dunking its flowers into the mud.

'Good on walls' – will only grow with the support and protection of a wall.

'Vigorous' – rampantly invasive.

'Dainty' – small and insignificant.

'Muted shades' – devoid of colour.

'A plant of character' – neither pretty nor shapely, it just looks peculiar.

'A wonderful plant for our warmer counties' – it won't survive any winters at all north of Penzance.

'Subtle aroma' – scentless.

'Repeat flowering' – may provide a freak blossom or two in autumn.

'Flowers continuously all summer' – repeats in a damp year.

'Happy anywhere' – rampantly invasive.

'Striking' – hideously garish.

'A useful carpeting plant' – lethally invasive. Nothing can withstand its advances and the Ministry of Agriculture are considering it as a noxious weed.

'Prefers a little peat for best results' – will only grow in some parts of County Kildare.

'An excellent plant of creeping habit' – rampantly invasive.

'An unusual plant' – looks peculiar. That's why nobody else sells it.

'Reliable' – boring. Everybody's got one.

'Indispensable and reliable' – There's one growing outside every bus shelter in the British Isles.

'Seldom offered' – difficult to propagate and impossible to keep alive.

'Semi evergreen' – looks a tatty mess in winter but you won't know whether to cut it back or not.

'An unusual colour combination' – ugh!

'We are proud to be able to offer this new introduction' – we will be charging three times the normal price for this plant until a competitor gets it into their catalogue.

'We are proud to be able to offer limited stocks of this new introduction' – the same as above except it's ten times the price.

'Easy' – rampantly invasive.

'With the familiar pungent aroma' – it smells awful.

One of the most difficult things for a catalogue composer to produce is a truthful colour description. You never read that a plant has red flowers or cream and pink petals. White doesn't exist. It has to be 'dazzling white' or 'purest white' or 'creamy white'. Reds are 'exciting vermilion' or 'vivid scarlet' or 'rich rosy red'. Orange and peach colours are 'warm, glowing orange' or 'elegant pale peach'. Blues are usually 'intense' or 'cool, ice blue' or 'azure'. Actual names of colours are often avoided altogether. 'Magenta' is used for anything from pinkish purple to black; 'carmine' is another favourite which vies with 'cerise' for pink or red tints. Why say 'yellow' when you can talk about 'gold' or 'rich golden' or, at the other end of the yellow band, 'lemon' or 'lemon cream'. Of course, conveying a sense of colour with mere words is nearly as inaccurate as showing colour photographs. One actually has to see the living plant to get a true idea of its colour.

Various attempts to make colour descriptions more objective have failed. The Royal Horticultural Society has made a valiant stab at the problem by producing an amazingly comprehensive colour chart which has about 800 shades all arranged on a series of fans which you flick open at the appropriate point. To make comparison easier, there is a hole in the middle of each colour patch. The idea is not to poke the stalk of the flower through the hole but to hold the petals underneath and look at them through the hole so they are surrounded by the synthetic colour. The trouble is, each petal, when you really look, has about 30 different colour shades on it. Furthermore, this *mélange* of hues alters as the flower fades. By the time you have picked your three 'average

'With the familiar pungent aroma.'

blooms, just fully open', according to the instructions, and worked out how to operate the fan in one hand without squashing the samples with the other, the flowers have faded and changed colour. Rule three on the instructions seems to be a sound one: 'Never attempt to match colours if the eye has become fatigued.' This fatigue usually happens long before you have finished working out which of the fans will match the flower you are holding. Take three people and they'll give you three different answers. Imagine how a catalogue would read if the RHS colour chart were used for the descriptions:

Geranium pratense   A perennial growing to about 45 cm with flowers 3 cm across, petals 93C fading to a paler 80D at their centres. Leaves, finely cut 146A.

Though it has its limitations, the RHS colour chart is incredibly useful for matching up colour schemes if you want to decorate your house. At over £20 for all those shades, it has to be something of a snip.

With your own catalogue, you must remember that whatever you write will be open to misinterpretation. The rule is, and this applies to all writing, that if ever two meanings can be extracted from one sentence, the wrong one will invariably be taken. You may think you have made things clear but there will always be a number of misinterpretations. After all, *double entendre* is the basis for most British humour – that's why the technique has a French name. These misunderstandings are always worse when you are writing down details like your opening hours. If you write 'Open daily from nine to five. Closed all day Monday', you will be plagued by visitors every Monday who will say: 'Well, it says here "Open daily" ' and will conveniently overlook the bit about being closed. But write 'Open six days a week, closed Monday', and some will assume you are only open on Mondays. The fact is, most people dislike reading. The eyes glaze over after the first few words in a block of text, so you have to assume that only a tiny fraction of what you write will be read and understood. In fact, I'm surprised you've got this far in the book – most people would have given up ages ago. Bully for you!

As well as giving out details of your hours, terms of trading and so on, most catalogues begin with a chatty introduction. This gives the budding authors a chance to rabbit on a bit, and is generally read by other catalogue producers to see how many grammatical mistakes they can spot. The usual form is for the nursery to congratulate itself on having an even bigger selection in spite of one of the most difficult growing years they've ever experienced. They will also say how clever they've been, managing to keep their price increases down to 30 per cent despite spiralling costs. There will be a special plug or two, especially for plants they've over-produced, and a plea to customers to get their orders in as early as possible.

Having got your preamble and terms sorted out, you are ready to begin writing your main text. Remember to do the hardest selling job on plants you want to get rid of most. Readers of catalogues may base their decisions on the tiniest suggestions, so don't be surprised if the plant you nearly removed from the list altogether, because you only had twenty for sale, turns out to be at the top of everyone's list. Won't they be furious when they can't have it!

Because accurate interpretation requires almost as much skill as successful writing, the rest of this chapter is devoted to extracts from a typical nursery catalogue with the proper translation for each entry. Read through these entries and you'll soon have the skill needed for good catalogue writing.

Ajuga pyramidalis   *Handsome blue spires over nicely coloured foliage. Vigorous and easy, ideal for a shady spot.*
Real meaning: ferociously invasive, smothering everything in its path. It has 9-inch spikes of bluish flowers that don't last in water. Short flowering season. Tolerates shade.

Chrysanthemum haradjanii   See *Tanacetum densum.*

Crocus ochroleucus   *A dainty cream crocus to cheer up those dark days in November.*
Real meaning: so small and weedy that you'll need about a thousand corms to see anything at all. The slightest breeze will damage the frail petals irreparably. Mice love them.

Daphne odora 'Aureomarginata'   *A noble shrub with waxy evergreen leaves, each with a delightful golden edge, and deliciously perfumed flowers in spring. Good for a sheltered wall or courtyard.*
Real meaning: the most frustrating of all the daphnes and not half

as pretty as many of the easier ones. In much of Britain, half the leaves fall off before the end of winter, leaving tatty stems. Provided there are no frosts beyond the end of February, you might get a greenish-white flower or two. Does very well in Cornwall.

Erigeron mucronatus   *A delightful little daisy, pale pink in the bud opening white and fading to pink again. Ideal for growing in dry walls or between paving slabs.*
Real meaning: very pretty but an absolute scourge. Seeds *everywhere*, popping up between cracks in your paths, walls, doorsteps, etc. The roots go down to Australia and, once established, nothing can eradicate it.

Funkia   see *Hosta*.

Fothergilla monticolor   *Handsome bottle-brush flowers, rich creamy white. In autumn the bush comes alive with a magnificent display of sunset colours. Prefers peaty soil.*
Real meaning: won't grow anywhere except on shaded, acid soil. The flowers are little off-white tufts. If you're lucky enough to get a decent clone it colours up quite well in autumn. Dull as ditchwater all summer.

Haematopus ostralegus   *Oyster Catcher. A fine Audubon print, in good order but with a slightly cracked frame* – Whoops, sorry, wrong catalogue.

Geranium phaeum   *The dusky cranesbill. Lovely spotted foliage above which come the deep magenta purple flowers with their elegantly swept-back petals in May.*
Real meaning: sometimes this plant has spotted leaves. The flowers are very small and often a dirty purple colour. It is invasive and has an unpleasant smell but is of limited use in natural woodland plantings.

Hebe 'Midsummer Beauty'   *One of the few really tough hebes which will sail through most winters with flying colours. The pointed leaves are reddish beneath. The flowers are long, decorative and lavender purple. In full bloom from midsummer to Christmas.*
Real meaning: just as infuriating as all the other hebes. It'll get through a couple of winters and then, just when you've become

really attached to it, five degrees of frost will finish it off, leaving you with a horrible hole in your planting scheme.

Hosta   see *Funkia*.

Inula hookeri   *A vigorous perennial, happy in any reasonable soil. The rich golden daisy flowers, their petals arranged in elegant whorls, appear in late summer and last for weeks.*
Real meaning: a rampantly invasive weed which, though quite showy, lasts about a week and needs careful staking to prevent collapse.

Juglans regia   *The traditional walnut. A wonderful tree, not nearly as slow as you might think, which produces a heavy crop of delicious walnuts. Try pickling the young green fruit in June. Mmm! Tasty!*
Real meaning: plant now and your great-grandchildren will either thank you for the first crop of nuts or curse you because you planted it too damn near the house and they feel they can't cut it down in case you turn in your grave and send down a murrain on their chickens.

Kniphofia 'Buttercup'   *An outstanding red hot poker with warm yellow flowers on 3-ft stems in June and again in late August. Wonderful planted near* Buddleia *'Lochinch'*.
Real meaning: quite a decent flower on the whole, but dear Lord! those dreadful leaves! Flopping about all over the place making the whole area within 10 yards of the plant look a mess. Notice how they cut interestingly into your flesh when you try to claw them out with your bare hands. Not fully winter hardy.

Lavatera olbia 'Rosea'   *A spectacular shrub with huge arching branches smothered for months with silvery pink blossoms. One of the finest plants to be introduced in recent years.*
Real meaning: actually, it was introduced before 1920 but has recently enjoyed a garden centre hype. You'll see it in every front garden, often rubbing shoulders with such unlikely bedfellows as yellow hypericum and red roses – probably 'Superstar' q.v. In the right spot, cut back to the ground every year, it makes a goodish plant, but is perhaps a bit, well, you know, naff, for some of our more erudite gardening experts.

Meconopsis betonicifolia   *The mysterious blue poppy from the*

Himalayas. A succession of cool blue poppy flowers with golden stamens. Loves shade. An aristocrat among plants.

Real meaning: this beautiful plant is next to impossible to grow and invariably kicks the bucket when it has flowered once. You need to collect seed, sow it in wet compost and stand the pan in the deep freeze for one week and the bottom of the fridge for five weeks. If you have managed to do this without incurring the wrath of your spouse you have either a very understanding spouse who is also a keen gardener, or a slovenly household. Shape up at once!

Nepeta govaniana   A plant of great character, freely branching with nettle-like leaves and soft creamy yellow flowers which are curiously lobed. Flowers constantly from July to October.

Real meaning: a dreary plant, reminiscent of a dead nettle but without its charm. Too wishy-washy to show up much but currently championed by the greenery-gallery brigade. Hates sun.

Ophiopogon planiscapus 'Nigrescens'   An intriguing and distinctly beautiful black-leaved glass-like member of the lily family.

Real meaning: one of the worst things to happen to British horticulture was that the landscapers got hold of this plant and put it everywhere. It has the charm of shredded black polythene and grows at about the same pace. The flowers, if they ever appear, are so tiny and boring they are not worth waiting for. A truly hateful child of our time, going as it does with fake stone and concrete cobbles. There is a green form which is equally undesirable.

Polygonum baldschuanicum   A wonderfully easy climber smothered with waxy white blooms all summer. Ideal for covering unsightly walls or fences.

Real meaning: Russian bindweed (they'll often omit the English name). One of the most disastrous introductions to our garden flora. Rampaging over every obstacle, however high or wide, this plant will reduce any garden of less than 10 acres to a wilderness of tangled stems within a couple of years. The only reward for all this is a show of nondescript, off-white flowers in summer. A good subject to plant *after* you have sold your house.

Quercus frainetto   A fine oak from eastern Europe whose huge lobed leaves turn golden yellow in autumn.

Real meaning: you thought all oaks were slow didn't you? This one, which you've planted a yard or two from your neighbour's bathroom window – so they can't spy on your private shenanigans – makes poplar look like bonsai. They'll be on to you about its roots breaking their pipes within the year. By the way, the leaves just turn brown and drop off.

Rudbeckia purpurea   see *Echinacea*.

Rose 'Superstar'   *This rose caused a sensation when it was introduced in 1960. The bright vermilion was a new and unique colour to roses and it remains today a truly spectacular plant.*
Real meaning: nobody realised to what depths of depravity plant breeders could sink until this monstrosity was launched onto the British market where, with their unerring taste, the gardening public fell on it with more gusto and enthusiasm than had previously been considered possible. The red/orange, dayglo blooms go with nothing else apart from the green of the garden gnome's trousers. Furthermore, by mid-July every year 'Superstar' is smothered with powdery mildew.

Sternbergia lutea   *One of the most enchanting autumn-flowering bulbs. The flowers are cup-shaped, golden yellow and produced without leaves in October.*
Real meaning: it doesn't matter how many times or at what expense you buy these lovely bulbs from the merchants, the same thing happens year after year. You plant 50. Three flower and the following season there is no trace, which makes you wonder whether you really did plant them or whether it was all a dream. Your friends in Dorset have them all over the garden, but that only serves to increase your frustration. This same description fits

Zephyrantes, Amaryllis belladonna and about 700 other exotic autumn bulbs that you long to have. You'd even give up all those scruffy colchicums for one healthy clump of crimson nerines, wouldn't you?

Tanacetum densum   see alpine section.

Trillium grandiflorum   *American wake robin. A wonderful plant that revels in moist woodland, spreading rapidly from underground runners. Pure white, three-petalled flowers that flush pink with age. 1 ft, spring.*
Real meaning: this is as bad as the last entry. If you live on cool, acid soil, preferably in the middle of a dense forest, this plant will

grow like twitch for you. The rest of us have to struggle to squeeze a single flower out of a root that has been crouched over for half a decade. You only have to think 'lime' and it will die by telepathy. This is doubly galling if you have ever romped gaily through North American woods that were a carpet of white trilliums for the whole of May.

Uvularia grandiflora   *Straw-coloured blooms of great elegance in woodland conditions.*
Real meaning: sounds anatomical. Won't grow.

Viburnum × bodnantense   *Everyone knows the beauty of this winter-flowering shrub. Fragrant sprays of pink flowers from December to March.*
Real meaning: what they don't tell you is that the thing is hideously ungainly and dull from April to November. Sparrows love the buds – those that the bullfinches have left.

Weigela florida foliis purpureis   *Wonderful dark-leaved form of the familiar shrub. The shapely flowers are glowing pink.*
Real meaning: another black-leaved horror, but at least the flowers are quite pretty. While we're on the subject, there's a black-leaved birch, a dead-looking elder and a dogwood with black stems – all horrible and best avoided like the plague.

Zygadenus   *Member of the lily family having grassy foliage with pretty white flowers.*
Real meaning: boring woodland plants but one has to have something beginning with a Z for the sake of completing the catalogue.

By now, you should be well on in your quest to become a truly great gardening expert. Here are a few simple exercises to enable you to assess your progress so far:

1 Your neighbour wants to get hold of some old-fashioned perennial wallflowers. Do you advise her to (**a**) visit a garden centre; (**b**) send away for them from a specialist nursery; (**c**) steal cuttings from a garden open to the public; (**d**) scrounge them from a TP; or (**e**) send for seed from a specialist society.

The answer is (**d**) because (**a**) and (**b**) won't have them, (**c**) is beyond the pale and (**e**) is wrong because named clones can't be

What does a pile of 4,000 catalogues look like?

grown from seed. But you wouldn't want your neighbour to have them anyway, so you'll probably send her to the wrong source.

2 Do you declare which catalogues you use?

This is tricky. Some are status-worthy. Others are not really acceptable as sources of plants among experts even though they all deal with them in secret from time to time. The same goes for market stalls – buy in secret, pretending the plants are for an ignorant friend.

3 Which is the most exciting and fruitful source of interesting plants? (**a**) Woolworths; (**b**) specialist nurseries; (**c**) garden centres; (**d**) flower shows; (**e**) societies; (**f**) granny?

The answer is none of the above. The best source ever is the plant stall at any local Women's Institute market. You never know what to expect, but you will never be disappointed.

4 What does a pile of 4,000 catalogues look like? How much is second-class postage on that lot? Did you know they each weigh more than 60 grammes so the cost to you in *extra* postage will be £200? By the way, the total weight is 280 kilos – much more than you can carry in your car. Have you imagined what the face of the man at the post office will look like when you say, 'Fourteen pence stamps, please.'

'How many?'

'Three thousand, nine hundred and seventeen, please.' Still, with all that coinage from your flower show catalogue sales, you'll be able to give him the right change!

Still want to go on?

Chapter 6

Open to the Public

'The unkindest cut of all . . . comes from those visitors who "would be so delighted to see our garden!" '
(Dean Reynolds Hole, *Our Gardens*, Dent 1899)

Telephone conversation in late spring:

'My name's Colborn, how can I help you?'

'Are you anything to do with the gardening?'

'Something of that sort, yes.'

'This is the Much Pethering WI here. We'd like to visit the gardens next year. When is the best time to come?'

'Late June. Or early July, when all the old-fashioned roses are at their best.'

'Oh dear! That wouldn't suit our members at all. We thought later.'

'Well, there is always plenty to see, whenever you come.'

'We thought an evening visit – about sevenish. Gives the members a chance to feed their husbands before they come.'

'What evening had you in mind?'

'We thought the fifteenth of October.'

'Well, we've nobody else booked for that evening. Are you sure that's when you want to come?'

'Yes, quite sure.'

'Will your members bring their own torches, or would you rather we rented floodlighting?'

'Oh, of course, it'll be dark then won't it? Well, perhaps our ladies would prefer to visit the bacon factory instead.'

Few people realise, before they do it, just how much opening their garden to the public can change their way of life. Every acclaimed gardening expert has to do it at some time and most of those who have allowed their gardens to enslave them have to open regularly to earn a few pennies so that they can keep going with their grand obsession. It doesn't really matter how small or big your garden is – although it might be regarded as ambitious to expect people to pay for the privilege of admiring your window box if that's all you have. Mind you, the great Gertrude Jekyll once prepared a detailed planting plan for a window box. History doesn't relate whether or not she charged a fee.

There are several ways of finding out whether your garden is ready to open up. A good idea is to visit other people's and observe what is special about theirs. You'll find the National Gardens Scheme, or 'Yellow Book', helpful in this respect. Don't worry too much about the Sissinghursts, Hidcotes and Nymans – they are huge and famous and are likely to be out of your league – but pick on a few 'Sunnysides', 'Dunrovans', 'Old Rectories' and 'Forge Cottages'. Some of these are certain to strike a common chord with you, and in any case will probably be better manicured than many of the great gardens are these days.

Most people expect to see plants in public gardens that do not grow in their own. If you haven't already, it will be necessary to plant a few rarities. You must have these properly labelled too. Leaving the nursery name tag on won't do. It's no bad thing to put the date of planting on the label and the plant's origin – no, not 'Hilliers of Winchester', but 'Szechuan' or 'Nepal'. As well as telling the visitors about the plant's origin, this practice also allows you to kid some of them that you actually went there to collect it yourself.

One final test is to invite your best friend over when everything is looking its best. Pick a day when the air is heavy with the scent of honeysuckle blossom, when your borders are a symphony of colour and when the roses over your door have pink, dew-specked buds. As you shepherd her round the best bits just say, quietly and in a non-committal voice: 'We thought of opening for the Red Cross.'

If she looks startled, does a little laugh with ever so tiny a note of scorn and says, 'No! Surely not. What is there to see?', you can be certain your garden is ready for the world. If she says, 'What a splendid idea, do say when I can tell everyone to come and support you,' you should stay private for another year or so.

Once you've made your decision you will need to decide

whether to donate part or all of your takings to charity. The Red Cross and National Gardens Scheme earn quite a lot from open gardens, but there are plenty of other ways of providing for deserving causes. Getting into the 'Yellow Book' is good if you're the type who needs his ego massaged from time to time. It's on general sale, so you can stroll into W. H. Smith when you're feeling a bit down and leaf through it to find your name in print. Extreme cases have been known to leave the books lying about the shop, all open at the appropriate page.

When your garden has been open for a year or two, you will start appearing in other guide books. The ultimate goal, however, is to become a red star in a road atlas. To achieve this you will have to apply for big yellow AA roadsigns – an expensive exercise but think of the points you will score when people you've invited for dinner telephone you for directions. Instead of all that confusing data like 'Right at the Dog and Bitch pub, left under the railway, straight over the roundabout, bear sharp right at the church, etc. etc.' you simply say 'Follow the signs!'

The style of entry in the guide books says much about the type of garden that is open. Nowadays, when the public has access to so many, it's vital to get your entry right. This is difficult when you are expected to convey all the joy, colour, scent and fascination of your garden in about twenty words. Here are a few examples pinched from a yet-to-be-published popular guide:

HAMPSHIRE   Mullion House, Lower Piddocks
Col. & Mrs H. St J. Lorne-Groomer
Just over an acre of walled gardens with herbaceous borders, fine collection of shrubs, old roses and immaculate lawns. (Public not allowed on the lawns.) Teas, in aid of the vicar's organ fund.
Admission: Adults 50p. Children £4.50. No dogs.

YORKSHIRE   The Old Shippon, Lonelydale
Dr Anthony Rockfreak
A 300-square-foot wonderland of rare alpines set in the side of Lonelydale rock (900 feet above sea level). Collections of gentians, saxifrages and Icelandic natives, many collected in the wild by the owner.
Admission: 75p. AGS members free. Climbing irons and rope recommended. Tufa culture classes given in spring.

SURREY   27 Mafeking Road, Caterham
Sid and Gladys Oddbod
Small suburban garden completely devoted to bedding plants and fuchsias. See the pink and yellow tulips in spring followed by an amazing display of scarlet salvias, purple petunias and orange African marigolds in July. Lily pond and gnomes.
Admission: 25p. OAPs free. Fuchsias and home-made gnomes for sale.

GLOUCESTERSHIRE   The Dower House, Tumbling in the Marsh
The Dowager Duchess of Genera
Nine acres of plantsman's paradise. Rose gardens, large collection of camellias, stream and water gardens. Home of the famous Roald Oak (Quercus dahliensis), *which acted as a landmark for Cromwell's army, hid Charles II and from whose branches the scurrilous witches of Hatchabog were hanged in 1652.*
Admission: £1.50. Rare plants for sale (nothing less than £19.99 – pot not included).

DORSET   Valerian Cottage, Little Piddle
Miss Emily Nostalger
Delightful cottage garden stuffed with old-fashioned plants (and silver bells and cockleshells too). The owner will give you a history of every flower. Most of them were handed down from her grandmother (the famous Gertrude Nostalger, author of A Dorset Lady Gardener's Jottings). *Fine collection of lavenders and sweet violets.*
Admission: 53p, third Sundays only, 2 to 6. No children. Cats welcome.

OXFORDSHIRE   The Old Rectory, Chipping Rarsbury
Mr & Mrs Freddie Nulyposch
In 1982, when the present owners bought the rectory, the old gardens were bulldozed away to make room for the tennis courts, swimming pool and sauna. Mexican landscapers were brought in to advise. The rocks and cacti contrast interestingly with the elegant line of the house (built 1784) but the huge solarium is the garden's main attraction, populated as it is with palms, tropical ferns and Swedish masseurs.
Admission: 50p. (Massages £35 per hour – or more, depending on your tastes.) Proceeds to the Millionaires in Debt Fund.

DEVON   Buzzacott Farm, Harriet Becherstowe
Tom and Betty Thornprufe
Not so much a garden as a wildlife sanctuary. Don't expect to see hybrid tea roses, delphiniums or a patio here. However, if you long to observe ravens cracking mussel shells, hedgehogs stalking adders or Duke of Burgundy fritillary caterpillars devouring cowslips, this place is for you. Bring your binoculars.
Admission: £1.00. Proceeds to World Wildlife and Tweeds in Distress. No twitchers.

The Clochemerle Syndrome

One fine and busy Sunday, when I was trying to hand weed a border and keep an eye on the visitors (see section on klepto-maniacs) at the same time, I detected a customer lurking at the periphery of my vision, a yard and a half from my left shoulder. I straightened up, composing a 'so-pleased-you-could-honour-us-with-your-presence' smile, and looked straight into the severest pair of steel-framed spectacles I have ever seen. The face was fixed with a puzzled frown and topped with a black beret. 'A keen plantsman,' I thought. 'I bet he's going to tick me off for having something labelled wrongly.' I said 'Good afternoon' as politely as I could, but the specs merely glinted in the sunlight.

'I'm confronted with something of a conundrum,' said the beret.

'Regius Professor of Philsophy,' I thought. 'A don at any rate, if ever I saw one.'

'Oh?' I replied, cautiously.

'It's your downpipes,' continued the don, indicating the house with a minuscule twitch of the spectacles.

'Yes?'

'There are more than one. All different ages.'

'That's right.' I was truly foxed by now. Not only was it an odd query but his English wasn't up to Oxbridge standards either.

'Am I to conclude, therefore, that there is more than one water closet in the house?'

'Possibly,' I countered. This was becoming personal.

'At this end', he continued – there was no stopping him now –

'two downpipes lead into one. Yet on your west elevation – I assume it to be west if your house is to the east of the London to Edinburgh railway line – there are more downpipes. Exactly how many closets exist in the house?'

'As many as we need.' I was beginning to feel resentful but the glasses flashed once more.

'I deduce that you have four.'

'Ah?'

'I believe I'm right. Unless some of the pipes are rainwater goods. Thank you for your assistance. A most interesting afternoon.' And with that he wandered off to retrieve his companion who was behind a laurel bush, trying to look as though she didn't belong to him.

Why is it that we never discover serious flaws in our plans until too late? I suppose the art of being a Montgomery or a Nelson amounts to no more than foreseeing all the pitfalls in time to change tactics. Overlook a single one and you're in trouble. Once the public has been let loose in your garden, you are likely to run up against a whole batch of unexpected brain teasers. One of the biggest mistakes we made was to underestimate the importance of providing a top quality lavatory.

We first opened up in 1982 for just one isolated afternoon. We hoped, because of such a short opening period, that people would not expect us to provide 'facilities' at all. How wrong we were.

'Have you got a toilet?' asked an embarrassed father whose four-year-old son was dancing from foot to foot clutching his waterworks with a heroism that belittled the Dutch boy and the dyke.

'Wouldn't your little boy like to nip into the shrubbery?' I suggested. The father was visibly shocked.

'Are you saying there are no facilities?' he asked, looking at me as if I were a convicted child molester.

'Well, we're only open today. It would have been a bit expensive to lay on a lavatory just for one afternoon don't you think?'

'But my boy's in agony.'

'Well, you could take him into that field. There are plenty of trees there.' The father glared at me and put on a wheedling voice for the child.

'Have you got a toilet?'

'D'you want to go behind a tree, Sonny?' The child clutched himself even harder and shook his head.

'Don't want to,' he whined. 'Want a proper toilet.'

'You'd better use our private loo,' I said, showing them the way and watching the growing trail of muddy footsteps on the carpet. I could see that next year, when we opened regularly, we would have to do something about the 'lavatorial situation'.

It was my father-in-law who came to the rescue. 'Why not borrow our Elsan?' he said. So on our next trip to Norfolk we collected the necessary apparatus, with about a year's supply of the special chemical, and rattled our way home. Why are lavs so funny? Why, in the busiest car park in Peterborough, did it make such a loud noise when it fell out and rolled across the concrete, shedding its seat as it went?

The next problem was where to site it. 'In the barn,' I suggested.

'Too draughty,' countered my wife. 'Besides, you can't lock the door.' We finally decided on an ex-loose box in the stables. Being the size of an average bedroom in a stately home, it made the Elsan look small and somehow rather pathetic, sitting in the middle. We replaced the half door with a whole one – more private – and set up a sink and pannikin, a bar of soap and a clean towel. Within a week mice had eaten the soap. I tried a brand with stronger perfume. They didn't like it. It took them two weeks to finish it. Later, when they'd lost interest in the soap, they started on the light flex, chewing right through both wires and causing a bright blue explosion. After that it seemed easier to knock a hole in the wall and build a high window to provide natural light.

We made a notice that said LAVATORY, nailed it to the door and hid in a nearby building to see how the customers would react. Some of them went in and came out, evidently relieved, without making a comment. Some burst into laughter. One group loved it. The women went in first, amid shrieks of laughter, and after them the men who said things like, 'Ha ha, I like it . . . but not a lot' and 'Oh cripes, a dinkum dunny! Reminds me of home!' Which proves we've had at least one overseas visitor.

Others were less amused. One lady arrived in extreme discomfort, having driven for a hundred miles. She asked for the loo and disappeared into it, emerging a nanosecond later, crimson to the roots of her blue rinse.

'I'm afraid I'm not used to that kind of thing,' she said. We took pity and let her into the house. Someone else said: 'Your toilet's a disgrace. Pity really, because it's such a lovely garden.'

Although the Elsan got us out of a spot, the lack of plumbing made things very awkward. The last straw was when, carrying a very full bucket, I tripped. It took several baths before I felt truly clean again. We decided to come up with something a little more *convenient* for the following year. I got the name of a local hero who hires out portable buildings including lavatories. For a mere £12 per week, we were told, we could have a proper flushing loo in its own little cabin, complete with wash basin and running water.

'What about planning permission?' I asked.

'Most of my customers don't bother,' said the local hero.

'Still, I'd rather be all legal and above board and that,' I said. (Local hero regarded me with new suspicion.)

'It's up to you,' he muttered.

The next step was to involve the planning authorities. When we came to this garden, there was a grotty little paddock by the road which was being used as a dump by the outgoing farmer. It took us most of our first winter to clear up the rotting wood, rusting pieces of agricultural machinery, broken mangers, irrigation pipes and piles of rocks. Once cleared, we re-seeded the area, planted a hundred or so trees of various species and renovated the mangled iron fence. Once we had decided to open the garden to the public, we set this newly beautified area (about 3 acres) aside as a picnic zone, fencing off a generous chunk for visitors to park their cars. Besides our new plantings, several mature trees grow there, so it seemed sensible to us to site a lavatory near these and to grow a screen round it so that it was discreetly hidden from view but readily accessible for our customers.

The planning officer thought that a good idea too. The planning committee thought differently. They decided, without the benefit of having visited the site, that it would detract from the amenity value of the village. The idiocy of this decision infuriated me. It seemed crazy that as a farmer, I am able, without any reference at all to the planning authorities, to erect a vast building of up to 5,000 square feet and as high as I like, in full view of the rest of the village. I may not, however, place a tiny temporary cabin, however well screened by trees and hedge, in my customers' picnic area.

Visitors to our gardens nowadays have to walk a quarter of mile down past our southernmost boundary to spend a penny. Once there, they can enjoy rural isolation in a sentry box complete with wash basin and running water. Being galvanised iron, the cabin gets up to about 120°F on a hot day. When we have closed up at the end of the day, I always throw a handful of gravel at it. Inside, the sound of the stones striking the metal wall is like the closing bars of the 1812 Overture and will be sure to *flush* out any lingerers.

If we had given proper and careful thought to the lavatory requirements of the general public, we might have decided against opening up at all. When you look into the possibility of opening your garden, never forget that there is no stronger stimulus to the bladder than discovering the absence of a convenience.

Blood Money

Almost without exception, the admission fees to gardens in Britain are far too low. Costs of maintenance are so incredibly high that it is difficult to imagine how some owners raise enough money to pay a part-time gardener, much less to keep renewing stock, maintaining structures and expanding collections. The tradition of undercharging seems to stem from the charitable nature of most garden-opening exercises. However, as a commercial activity, opening up is a non-starter unless you work out your costs and charge a realistic sum for entry. You try explaining that to your customers! Some of their comments still ring in my ears:

'Beth Chatto only charges 50p and her garden is much better than yours!' (No doubt true, but the person who said this had never seen our garden.)

'A pound is too much just to look at a garden.'

'Do we get our money back if it rains?'

'Why do you charge to see the garden if you sell plants as well?'

'We've been before. Do we have to pay again?'

After a while, one begins to feel guilt-ridden about even so much as inviting folk to part with a few bob. Even if, in return, they can spend several hours among a collection of 3,500 different species and varieties of plants from all over the world, laid out in a peaceful and rural setting. ('Rural' does not automatically mean 'peaceful' – have you sat in a garden bordered by fields in which nine combine harvesters are running? Or listened to the salvoes of cannon keeping pigeons off oilseed rape crops?)

You will need to give your admission policy lots of careful thought but, whatever you decide, be prepared for the odd moan. If you have groups visiting, it is helpful to persuade their leader to collect up the entry fees before they arrive. I have found myself handing a tin round for everyone to drop in a pound coin. It's terribly embarrassing to have to ask who is missing a button later on, when you have had a chance to empty out the tin.

Dealing with . . .

Children

As a nation, we British seem to dislike children intensely. Adults who are beyond childbearing age often shun them like the plague. One seldom sees a mature Englishman spontaneously throwing his arms round a small child in the way that, say, a warm-hearted Italian would. As far as gardens are concerned, eminent experts have been heard to say that children and gardens don't mix. This simply isn't true. My four children have all led boisterous, happy lives in our garden and have perpetrated considerably less damage in a dozen years than a casual gardener could do in half a day. (They've ruined the house, but that's another story.)

Training children not to wreck a garden is exactly the same as training a dog. If you shout 'OFF!' in a threatening way when either dog or child strays onto a forbidden zone, like rockery or flowerbed, they soon learn to keep off. The problem arises when other people's children are doing the damage. Parents get very narked if you start bellowing at their children, but seldom take action themselves to stop them misbehaving. It is important to stress, before going any further, that the great majority of children who visit us are perfectly delightful. One always remembers the odd hooligan rather than the host of little angels.

Each age of child brings its own set of problems. Tiny babies' prams get wheeled across the corners of the mixed borders. Toddlers are inclined to pluck flowers off (but are not nearly as bad for that as certain types of adult visitor) and fall over a lot. They don't usually hurt themselves but make a terrific din, making one think they have, at the very least, broken a couple of ribs. Bright berries are a big worry, especially to toddlers' mothers. We have a fine clump of *Actea rubra*, or red baneberry, whose glistening crimson fruits are irresistible to little questing fingers. They are fairly poisonous, and so was a particular child I saw last August. It was about to gobble up a generous handful of them, having already pulled the buds off several lilies. The temptation *not* to grab its arm and warn its mother was a difficult one to resist. She seemed blissfully unconcerned, even when I told her how dangerous they were. Luckily, before there were any casualties mistle thrushes ate the rest of the baneberries.

Primary-school-age children usually lark about and appreciate an area where they can do this without disturbing the other customers. Don't be alarmed if you find them at the top of your highest trees. Just remember that when they fall out and injure themselves, you are liable. If they are the children of American parents – a litigious nation that – you will almost certainly be sued for millions of dollars. Providing footballs, nature trails, adventure playgrounds and having a few animals about can help. Our trio of pet goats have kept youngsters amused for hours, especially when they have managed to get their parents to lean unwittingly against the electric fence.

Older children fall into two categories: the sullen, bored stiff variety and the prematurely budding plantsman. On the whole, the former is easier to deal with. Usually, before too long they have a row with their father or mother and go to sulk in the car. Others hang round their parents sighing loudly. They seldom do damage, although I once saw one distractedly tying the stems of a bamboo plant into knots. I couldn't tell whether it was boy or girl, for it had lank hair and was wearing a set of shapeless black garments including Uriah Heap mittens and leg muffs.

The premature budding plantsman is usually a right little know-all. They can be of either sex and often have a disconcertingly good knowledge of plants. This they are anxious to air and soon have you locked in an intense conversation about the comparative anatomy of *Primula* in the *vernales* section. 'Golly,' you think to yourself, 'this lad will be a True Plantsman one day – if he lives long enough.' It always reminds me of that sinister line from *Richard III* in which Richard, when the young prince is being stroppy, says: 'Short summers lightly have a forward spring.' We know what happened to him, don't we? Yes you do! In the tower – Tyrrel and all that cloak and dagger stuff.

Opening hours

Imagine six thirty on a Sunday evening in August. The last of several hundred visitors has just left and you are bringing in your GARDEN OPEN sign. In a few moments you will be able to bolt the door and collapse into a comfortable chair with a sizeable whisky and soda. Suddenly there is a squeal of brakes. A BMW pulls up and out jumps a smart woman in her fifties wearing a Thai silk dress and crocodile accessories.

'Thank God we're not too late!' she says as her partner emerges from the driver's side. You can tell by his rings and Gucci shoes that he's not exactly a pauper. Could these be the customers who will buy half your stock in a quick ten-minute whip-round? You think they might be.

'Do come in,' you say, flogging your tired face into yet another smile.

'Would you be an angel and show us the garden?' gushes the woman. And for some reason, because it's after hours perhaps, you not only let them in free, but you conduct them round the entire garden yourself. Personally. They fire questions at you. They admire a plant here, a colour combination there. They offer opinions on your lay-out and ask why you aren't better known. They go on to drop a few names: 'Roy Lancaster gave us a so and so. We do so love visiting Christopher Lloyd. Do you see much of Robin Herbert?'

By eight o'clock it's getting dusk and you shepherd them towards the plant-selling area.

'What a lovely selection you have,' they say and ask you to conduct them through the frames of plants for sale. By now your greed is developing nicely and you think they might go for at least a hundred quid's worth.

'Would you like a basket. Or a trolley?' you ask, hopefully.

'Lord no!' They both laugh. 'We've only a tiny courtyard. Just off Holland Park Avenue. I think we'll just take a couple of these little pansies. How much are they?'

'Eighty pence.'

'What, each? Perhaps we'll just have one.'

There will always be the earlybird too. If you open punctually at the appointed time, nobody will be there. The place will be deserted for at least another hour. But try sleeping late on a Sunday. Just be three minutes late throwing open the gates and you can depend on there being a frustrated customer pacing up and down the road outside as if you had kept waiting for three hours.

Rude remarks

Being a pretty mean deliverer of rude remarks myself, I have no right to complain about them when I am at the receiving end. However, many would-be gardening experts are sensitive souls, and knowing how to handle unkind comments can make life a lot less fraught. People can be surprisingly tactless and sometimes the verbal slap in the eye comes from a surprising source. Sweet little old ladies can be vitriolic on occasions and the most timid of creatures may suddenly turn on you if they are being taken for a ride. When you're open to the public you are considered fair game and it is imprudent to try to fight back.

After years of hard work I felt proud enough of our wild garden to show it to one of my smarter gardening friends. I stood beside her while we enjoyed the drifts of *Cyclamen coum,* primroses, violets, snakeshead fritillaries and wild daffodils. Emerald green bunches of ferny cow parsley leaves were unfurling and would provide a lacy canopy later on. Here and there the odd red dead-nettle, speedwell, celandine and dandelion enhanced the feeling of wildness. All she could say was: 'Mm. Nice flowers, shame about the weeds!'

Other visitors are wont to comment about the state of the house:

'Who lives in the house?'

'We do.'

'What are yer? Sort of caretakers?'

'Up to a point.'

'Well, yer stonework's a bit perished. When d'yer think the wood work'll get painted? Fancy letting it get to that state.' Sometimes people peer into the windows and actually comment on things they see inside the house: 'Nice bit of Staffordshire' or 'I bet that room's draughty in winter'.

One dear soul, from the West Midlands I suspected, arrived on a motorbike, paid his entry fee and stood in the middle of the first lawn. 'Oh' he said, 'what I could do with this garden. I'd pull all them shrubs out over there and plant a mass of "Whisky Mac" roses. I'd get rid of all them old perennials too, and flood the borders with bedding plants. I like plenty of colour, me.'

'But some of "them old perennials" are pretty rare,' I said.

He shook his head sadly. 'You've got to 'ave colour in a garden,' he said. 'This one's all green. Nothing bright.'

Another day a fan flagged me down as I passed the gravel scree where some of our smaller treasures reside. 'Excuse me,' she called, 'but it says in this guide that there are unusual plants here.'

'That's right,' I said.

'Well, where are they?'

'All round your feet.' She looked down at the *Delphinium tatsienense*, *Salix fargesii*, *Carex buchananii* and other rarities, thought for a while and then said: 'What's unusual about them?'

'Well,' I said 'they're not grown very commonly and come from remote parts of the world. That kingfisher-blue delphinium is a bit special, don't you think? It's such an intense colour and so compact.'

'Ah but it's not what I'd call unusual. You can get delphs anywhere. Much bigger than that too. Now my friend's got a pitcher plant. Ever heard of one of those? It eats flies. That's more unusual than anything you've got here.'

More discerning gardeners can floor one with a casual side swipe too. They use words like 'interesting', 'unfortunate', or 'strange'.

'That's a *strange* way to train a climbing rose,' said a friend looking at an 'Albertine' that had escaped its annual pruning and partly fallen off the wall.

'Unfortunate colour combination,' murmured another as he looked at a shock of scarlet and white opium poppies that had sprung up next door to the Beaujolais-coloured rose 'Mrs Anthony Waterer'.

'*Interesting* that you should have thought of putting tall stuff at the front and short at the back.' And so on. One simply has to take these remarks on the chin. If you're lucky enough to earn compliments and praise, this will usually neutralise the sting of the unkind comments.

Howlers can also help to provide comic relief. A charming shrub with tiny ruby flowers and glossy little leaves (*Fuchsia microphyllus*) grows on our terrace in a big terracotta pot. It flowers all summer and most people ask if we have the same plants for sale. One woman sidled up to me and said, 'Have you got a *microphallus*?' Of course, I wasn't about to give anything away!

The posh term for double flowers is *'flore-pleno'* or *'plenus'*. This is just Latin for 'full flower' or 'full'. A keen visitor wanted to get hold of some of our double lady's smock but when I noted down her needs, muttering as I wrote: 'Three *Cardamine pratensis flore-pleno'*, she interrupted with an 'Oh no! I've already got the plain form. I want the double from you.'

Overhearing a couple of very fashionable-looking persons in our rose garden, I was amused to hear one say to the other: 'The label says Rose "Ispahan" pre-1832 but I can't believe it's a hundred and fifty years old. It looks no older than the rose tree Dudley planted last winter.'

Queries and identifications

As a gardening expert you will often be called upon to identify plants for people. Frequently, one of our visitors will seek me out and describe a plant she has observed in the garden in such peculiar terms that I'm unable to develop the slightest idea of what she's on about. 'It's a red thing, like a delphinium,' she might say. 'You've got it growing by the wall' (we have about a thousand feet of wall) 'near the ground lilac.' To avoid further descriptions I usually drop what I'm doing and go to the spot with the customer. On arrival the plant will turn out not to be red, but pink, will be about as much like a delphinium as a walnut tree, and won't be growing anywhere near the walls. How the police manage to extract accurate descriptions from witnesses, heaven knows. When it comes to describing plants with any degree of accuracy, almost everyone has difficulty. Experts are no exception.

Most infuriating of all is the character who will come out of the garden with a handful of plucked-off pieces. Flowers, petals, leaves, sprigs will then be laid out and an identification of each demanded. One can ask the culprit not to pick the flowers but the answer is usually: 'Oh, but I've only taken tiny pieces.' The problem is that this sample-taking habit can spread and if 700 people pick a twig or two . . . well, you can see what I mean.

Kleptomania

One of the most attractive of the old single border pinks is a variety called 'Brympton Red' whose deliciously clove-scented flowers are deep red with crimson mottling. We acquired our first stock plant, quite legally, from Kiftsgate Court. (It's always useful to be able to let everyone know when you have collected a plant from somewhere posh like Kiftsgate, Sissinghurst or Great Dixter.) One day I emerged from our back door to see a tweedy gentleman bent double over the pink. At first I thought he was smelling the flowers, but he leapt to his feet saying: 'I was just tying my shoelace up.' That remark and the fact that his face was by now the same colour as the 'Brympton Red' pinks, suggested to me that he had been helping himself to some of my propagating material. When I looked at the young plant later on, as I expected, several cuttings had gone leaving nothing for me to propagate for the nursery.

There is a consensus that stealing from Woolworths is a criminal offence but snitching seed, cuttings or little pieces of plant is quite acceptable. High-ranking persons have, in the past, admitted to swiping cuttings from hotels, gardens, window boxes – in fact many have even boasted about it. If you accused, say, a judge's wife of knocking off a few grapes at the fruiterer's while she waited to be served, you'd probably land yourself in hot water. However, she may expect to be congratulated for 'acquiring' some seed of a rarity from a famous garden.

The problem becomes more embarrassing when one actually catches a thief – for that is what they are – red-handed. Far from being ashamed, many of them are indignant and regard your attitude as being petty-minded and vindictive. Occasionally, I have come across plants lying on the surface after cutting hunters have inadvertently uprooted them in their haste to grab a snippet. Certain plants are martyrs to this kind of attack. A strange-looking pansy called 'Irish Molly' with dusky, greenish-brown flowers on a yellowish background – it sounds awful but is really quite a charming little plant – seems to be much in demand. We are never able to take enough cuttings from our stock plants because certain members of the public beat us to them.

It may help to invite those who ache for a cutting of this or that to ask. The trouble is, you don't know who wants what. It certainly pays to have members of the family patrolling the more remote spots of the garden on busy days. One should never plant valuable treasures in secluded corners where a thief can commit the crime without fear of being disturbed. Some gardens suffer so badly from pilfering that they have been obliged to 'wire up' their more valuable items, causing alarm bells to ring as soon as they are touched.

(There's more on pilfering and how the expert criminals do it in the chapter on collecting on page 145.)

Coach Parties

Coach parties are an inevitable result of opening to the public. Some are great fun – especially groups of keen gardeners – others are frustrating. You soon find out that a sizeable section of the elderly population loves to cruise about in coaches. They have little interest in what goes on at the end of their journey but sign up for any tour that happens to be available, just for the ride. They are invariably brought by coach drivers who complain that you are hard to find and then give you a free business management seminar:

'Sorry we're an hour late, Gov. Couldn't find you.'
'Didn't you see the AA signs?'
'Well, yeah. But I couldn't find Peterborough to start with.'
'We're nowhere near Peterborough.'
'So we found out.'
'Did you look at your road map?'
'What road map. They don't supply us with road maps.'
'Well, how do you find your way about?'
'Boss tells us where to go. Only he's better on football grounds than garden centres.'

Toddlers are inclined to pluck flowers off and fall over a lot.

'This is *not* a garden centre.'

'Well, market garden then.'

'It's not a market garden either.'

'Oh? What is it then?'

'It's a garden. Quite a big garden. With a lot of interesting plants in it.'

'What's the point of that then?'

'It gives people pleasure.'

'What, 'n they pay a quid just to see a garden?'

'Indeed.'

'Don't see the point in it, mate! Not much of a money spinner anyway, is it?'

'Every little helps.'

'You know what you ought to do don't you?'

'No. What?'

'Get a bit more business-like. Set up some fruit machines, get a bar going, jazz the place up a bit.'

'Jazz up?'

'Yeah. Tell you what. Why don't you rig loudspeakers all over the garden and pipe music to the punters. Cheer things up a bit.'

'Got a driving licence have you?'

'What? 'course I have.'

'Why don't you go and get a professional driver to teach you how to drive safely and navigate properly?'

'What do you mean? What are you insinuating, mate?'

'I'm merely trying to tell you your job since you've been so keen to tell me mine, mate!'

Coach drivers are also experts on the shortcomings of 'they'. 'They' are the ones who should never have built the motorway so near London, should have never allowed tachographs to be fitted to lorries. 'They' should have brought back hanging years ago, should have sited the Kings Lynn bus station further away from the railway and should never have allowed Stan to erect his pigeon sheds in the front of the garden of number thirty one. Well, stands to reason, don't it, eh, mate!

On arrival, coach party members invariably head for the loos. Those at the back of the queue have just enough time to relieve themselves before getting back on the coach for the journey home. The other preoccupation with party visits are the teas. A garden tour, however fantastic the garden might be, is only made memorable if there was a tea – preferably with scones, clotted cream and strawberry jam. So, with the driver getting lost, loos, and teas and souvenir purchasing, there is little time for much actual garden watching.

Once you've decided to open up, certain changes will have to be made in your garden. Many of these will be highly inconvenient. The public won't want to pay to see your washing so the clothes line will have to go. My wife has developed quite strong arms and legs now from hiking a couple of hundred yards with every basket of washing. After much nagging and the exertion of extreme marital pressure, I managed to summon up enough energy to erect several poles and a line in a quiet part of the farm yard. I hadn't realised it was in the main flight path of all the sparrows in the parish – not to mention jackdaws, collared doves and starlings – so most of our sheets have to be washed two or three times. However, carrying them to and fro provides us, well, my wife, with plenty of valuable exercise.

You will have to provide garden seats – more than you'd need for your own family. Many avid garden visitors are infirm and have to rest from time to time. If you don't have enough seats placed strategically about the place, the teenage visitors will have bagged all available bottom space and the old folk will be deprived. It's important not to make the seats too comfortable or you may get squatters who will set up for the day with thermos flasks and knitting and keep everyone else off. Slatted seats are best for this, as long as the slats are not too close together.

Checking your garden furniture for safety, at least once a day, is advisable. The antics of a party of middle-aged ladies intrigued me once when I noticed several of them sitting for a tiny moment on a cheap rustic seat we'd recently bought, and then leaping up with a little shriek. It turned out that a large nail was protruding dangerously and was taking its toll. Luckily, nobody got seriously hurt.

When you have been open for a while, you'll soon realise that having the public around is not all bad. Oh no sir! Not by any means. This year's cutting remark about a colour scheme is going to influence next year's planting plans – probably for the better. A great many visitors will be genuine experts whose comments and advice are almost always helpful. Plant enthusiasts, a big-hearted bunch on the whole, will frequently bring material in as gifts or swaps. Varieties that I have been trying to track down for years will suddenly turn up that way. One makes dozens of new friends among the many interesting characters who drop in to see what sort of a collection you have. When owners or administrators of eminent gardens arrive, the result can be a private view of their own patches with a chance to exchange plants, seeds and ideas. But, above all, nothing is more satisfying than sharing the fruits of your labours with like-minded souls. To bask in the glow of their appreciation is undoubtedly one of the nicest aspects of opening your garden. It is an essential part of the true expert's development.

Chapter 7

Lecturing

'There is a slight problem. I've . . . er . . . I've forgotten my slides.'

(Colborn, Melton Mowbray, 1985)

As your career in gardening expertise develops, you will be able to take part in all kinds of horticultural functions without feeling inferior or ignorant. Naturally, sooner or later you will be asked to give a lecture. The prospect of doing this frightens the living daylights out of normal people. However, if, like me, you are a budding plantsman and a chronic megalomaniac, addicted to the sound of your own voice, once bitten by the bug you will sit pining by the 'phone, waiting for invitations. Each morning you will scour your post, tossing bills and circulars aside to get at those promising-looking envelopes that might contain a commission.

Dear sir,
The committee of the Whartley-by-Skregthorpe and District Allotment Association wonder whether you would be willing to address the members on the night of 19th February 1990 at the village hall at 8.00 pm. Most of our members are interested in vegetable production for table and for showing. Can you oblige us?

Yours truly,
Ned Pocke, Secretary.

Not quite the 'Dear Sir, Her Majesty has instructed me . . .' you'd hoped for – the lined writing paper was a bit of a giveaway and anyway, there was no royal crest – but it's better than nothing. It's a commission and in any case, the drive up to north Yorkshire will be quite a little adventure really, although what those vegetable growers want with a talk on plant hunting in Nepal, goodness only knows! Perhaps they think you're a vegetable man.

Foolproof lecturing is quite an art. Doing the lectures them-selves is challenge enough. Getting invited to do it at all proves to be something of a poser to the average expert.

One day last winter my 'phone rang.

'Colborn here,' I said – using the brisk, efficient but anxious-to-help voice. 'How can I help you?'

'This is Mrs Fortinbras – from Durbridge University.'

'Oh yes,' my heart skipped a beat. 'Academics,' I thought. 'My favourite types! – lots of lovely expenses and a fat fee and possibly even a chance to dine in Hall.'

'We wanted a speaker for next spring. For our ladies' horticulture club.'

'Ye-es' – not so exciting. Bored academic wives talking flower arranging. Nobody's favourite!

'Are you free on the fifteenth of March?'

'I'll just consult my diary,' I lied. Counted to ten and rattled a page of the 'phone book near the mouthpiece. 'Now . . . let me see. Yes, I seem to be free.'

'Oh that's splendid. We'll look forward to that immensely. I'm sure you'll find it rewarding.'

'What about travel expenses? Durbridge must be nearly three hundred miles from here.'

'Oh, I don't think we can run to that.'

'Well, my fee will cover part of the cost but you are a very long way off.'

'Fee?'

'For the lecture.'

'I didn't realise you would expect a fee.' Mrs Fortinbras's voice developing a sinister edge, 'I'll have to discuss this with the committee. We'll come back to you.'

Needless to say, she didn't. The world is littered, it would seem, with people who will happily give up evening after evening of their time lecturing for the fun of it! Similar, I suppose, to those persons who will write for magazines for nothing, just to get a byline, or even go in for vanity publishing, where you actually *pay* to have your book published. If you intend to be a real expert, it is of paramount importance that you *never* speak for free unless it happens to be an address for your favourite charity. It's unprofessional to do it and drops the rest of us smartly in the mire. Is that quite clear? Good!

All gardening experts, whatever their field of specialisation, will be expected to give a lecture, demonstration or talk at some time in their lives. The object of this chapter is to help you be good at it and to make sure that, after every appearance, your public image is enhanced. You'd be surprised at how many of our great horticulturists are rotten speakers. Many are shy, others are so earnestly locked in to their subjects that they forget to leave a little room for the audience. It's all a matter of technique. Learn the first basic steps and you will not need to worry about drying up, stage fright or technical hitches.

How to Get Started

Let us assume that, since you have had your garden open to the public for a year, one or two people have put out feelers to see whether you would be able to give a talk. You have finally, and reluctantly, agreed to do a gig for the local Red Cross. 'It won't be a big audience,' says the organiser. 'Less than a hundred and fifty anyway.' This scares you rigid. You'd visualised a little room with about twenty people. But if you'd done any speaking before, you'd have known that a couple of hundred people make the job miles easier than twenty.

'Besides', continues your organiser, 'it will be by invitation, so only the wealthiest locals will be coming – no riff-raff.' Now you're really in a panic. But don't be. This simply means that it will be a 'fleece the rich' exercise and the people who come will only do so because they feel they ought to be seen there, and not because they are remotely interested in gardening.

Like most of the guests, the invitation cards will be thick and white and will say:

Lady Rose Hyppe-Sirroppe requests the pleasure of your company at a reception and gardeners' supper in the gardens of Rollingstone Hall on Friday, 10th June at eight thirty pm etc, etc.
Black Tie. Carriages 1 am.

This will be in posh lettering on the front of the card arranged so that the recipients can put them on their mantel shelves to maximise swanking opportunities: 'We're off to Rosie Syrroppe's on Friday. Such a saint. etc.' On the back of the cards it will say, rather more tersely: 'RSVP Tickets, £25 each.'

On the appropriate evening, the Hyppe-Sirroppe stately pile will look like a special auction for Rolls-Royces and BMWs. The guests will adopt a high profile during the reception at the beginning of the evening.

'Ralph, darling! Fancy your being here, with *poor* Tamsin confined to the maternity ward. And twins my dear. Did you insure?'

'Of course. I'm a name now.'

'What do you mean, darling, a name?'

'Lloyd's. It's what they call you when you join Lloyd's.'

'I didn't even know you were thinking of working for a bank. What about your farm? Ooh look there's Fiona Scapula! My God! She's wearing a bin liner. Even so, she's obviously all bum and bosom. Fiona – OO-ooh! Over here love . . . Fiona, darling, I *love* your dress. It's absolutely terrif. Makes you look really elegant. I say, haven't you lost weight? Do you know Ralph Cruste? He's just started working for Lloyds Bank.'

'Hullo you two. Of course, stupid, he's my cousin. It's Lloyd's anyway, not the bank – and not really work. Many congrats, Ralph. How's Tammie?'

'She's resting up ready for the homecoming tomorrow. Mummy's given us a whole case of Dom Perignon.'

'Is that your Porsche – the F reg one?'

'Ya.'

'Lucky swine. I wanted David to buy me one but he's hooked on Mercs.'

'How is David?'

'Bored stiff with merchant banking. Wants to retire. He's made enough now and I reckon he's getting to the age where he needs to watch his health a bit.'

'But he's only thirty-one!'

'Twenty-nine, actually. Well. You see what I mean?'

'Won't a hundred and fifty K a year be hard to give up?'

'But what about the Quality of Life?'

'Oh, ya. *So* important, I do absolutely agree, don't you, Gemma?'

'Oh ya. Abso*lutely*.'
'Ya.'
'Ya. Absolutely.'
'My God! Look! Talking to Lord Tenderloin!'
'Good Heavens! Is that Dominic?'
'Ya!'

But five minutes into your talk they'll be sleeping like babes. I don't mean they'll actually be snoring, but each will have put on a bright, attentive mask – eyebrows slightly lifted, a half-smile fixed. Behind the mask they'll be thinking about the FT index, the price of Canadian wheat, what short gilts are likely to be doing in a year's time, what that private patient will do when he finds out the wrong kidney was removed and whether that new bit of crumpet at the office – not the wiggly dark one, the statuesque blonde one with the tight skirt – might respond to an indecent suggestion or two. This kind of function is the easiest to do. It doesn't matter a fig what you say because nobody's listening. The engagement that will really put you on your toes will be addressing a small group of specialists in your own special subject. An evening of saxifrage talk with six collectors can be more draining than a physics exam.

The first requirement of any good speaker is *presence*. If you have any special peculiarities like having three arms or horns growing out of your head, you will command all the attention you need without really trying. Ordinary-looking folk, however, have to practise their presence until they can be sure of undivided attention the very instant they make it felt. Like playing the piano or riding a bike, developing presence is a skill. To acquire this skill there are certain daily exercises you must undertake. You should start tomorrow.

1 Rehearse to the mirror. Every morning, when you go into the bathroom, stand in front of the mirror, pull your tummy in (it's usually best not to do these exercises in the nude because you could be distracted). You'll be embarrassed anyway – especially when your partner walks in in the middle – but that's the whole point of the exercise. You are vaccinating yourself against big future embarrassments by feeding yourself small daily doses. Now, lift your chin, look yourself straight in the eye and say: 'Be-bop-a-lula. She's my baby!'

Now come on! That was a terrified whisper. The whole point of this exercise is to get you to be able to talk the most feeble twaddle in a clear and resonant voice, looking your audience straight in the eyes – in this case your own eyes in that mirror. I say, they're a bit bloodshot this morning aren't they? Are you hitting the whisky just a teeny bit hard do you think? (See **Vine eyes,** Chapter 2.) Are you ready? Again then:

'Da do ron ron ron, da do ron ron!' Mm. A little better but you should speak from lower down, like a bass singer who tries to make the sound come from the pit of his stomach. (Actually, the best gardening experts speak from a good deal lower than their stomachs.) Practise saying these and similar inanities every morning until you can boom out the words in ringing tones without cringing at all.

2 Once you have overcome the embarrassment of doing this at home, go to your local shopping centre, walk into Woolworths and say, as loudly as possible: 'Ladies and gentlemen! May I have your attention?'

Absolutely nothing will happen. Nobody will look up from their shopping; things will go on as before. The object of this exercise is to train you to catch and hold attention, remember. Now try saying something completely nutty.

'Ladies and gentlemen!' (as loud as you can, remember). 'Floggle poggle pillock wallies!' The result is nearly the same. The only reaction you get is that the shoppers closest to you go out of their way not to look you in the eye. You still have not grabbed much attention. But now, shout this: 'FLASHER!' The effect is instantaneous. A sudden silence, all heads turn, the security man strides over to you and the little old man you hadn't noticed in the raincoat behind Lampshades and Accessories faints dead away. The object of this lesson has been to show you how to think up some *ingenious* way of attracting attention to yourself. Once that initial summons has been made, the floor is yours. An added benefit here is that situations like this will help you to develop another ability, i.e., getting out of awkward situations.

3 Improve your skill with jokes. English humour is usually rooted in fairly basic biological functions. Such horrid, but vital necessities as reproduction, voiding waste and so on must never be alluded to directly so we use *double entendre* – 'Wind surfers do it standing up', 'Young farmers do it with sheep'. Some people hang a second meaning on whenever they can. It becomes a compulsive habit with them and can be funny occasionally but is usually infuriating after the first five minutes. The most frequently used device for this is the gardener and art mistress routine, although some prefer to use the actress and bishop.

'Hello Claude, what have you been up to lately?'

'Oh busy, busy. It's a job to fit everything in these days – as the bishop said to the actress, ha ha! What about you?'

'Oh not a lot. I haven't been feeling myself lately, not since my operation.'

'Why? What have they removed ha ha?'

'Gall bladder.'

'You're all right though. You can still function and everything – as the actress said to the bishop, ha ha!'

'Well, it's a bit hard sometimes.'

'As the bishop said to the actress, ha ha! What about your garden? Got it all planted?'

'No, I'm not really up to much. I start off in the morning with plenty of vigour but I can't keep it up for long.'

'As the bishop said to the actress, ha ha! You're lucky you can keep it up at all in your condition, ha ha ha!'

The quality of your jokes should vary according to the quality of your audience. Clearly, actress and bishop jokes are out of the question for learned gatherings of experts, but should do nicely for village garden society evenings. Funny stories are fine, as long as you make it quite clear from the start that you are about to tell a funny story and the audience is therefore expected to laugh. If you have to end it with 'and that was the punchline', you can be fairly sure it fell flat. Make up your own jokes if you can. Use material you've heard from someone else, and the chances are the audience have heard it before too. Subtle jokes are useful devices because, if the crowd laughs, you can congratulate yourself for extreme cleverness, but if there is no reaction you can comfort yourself in the knowledge that they are a bunch of cretins with less imagination than a broken hoe and by no means up to your superior intellectual prowess.

4 Know your audience. This is crucial. There is nothing an audience hates more than being talked down to – nothing, that is, except being unable to understand a word the speaker says. Thus, if it is an inexpert audience you will have to make sure you appear as ignorant as they are. No scientific names, no difficult words. If you are among clever horticulturists and are unsure of your material, water it down a little with plenty of qualifying statements like 'reckoned to be' or 'up to a point' or 'there are those who believe'. Without saying a word, your audience will tell you all about how well you are doing. If they are silent and still, but clearly awake, you're probably being very boring. One person slipping out may mean she's about to throw up – no problem of yours, it was the mussels she ate for lunch – but if half the audience are sneaking out bent double, there's probably something wrong with your delivery. If they laugh at the right bits and you can keep catching the eye of any one of them as you talk – well done you!

Foreign audiences are different. Frequently, their skill in English is well up to understanding most of what you say, but with foreign audiences *never* try any jokes. They will always misfire and cause confusion. By the way, when you talk to foreigners, turning up the volume won't improve their understanding one jot. Frequently, when one sees English people abroad struggling on the wrong side of a language barrier, they try to get through by shouting and gesticulating a lot.

'El beacho, por favor!'

'Que señor?'

'La costa, LA MER. PEDALOES?'

'Que?'

'EL BEACHO S'IL VOUS PLAIT. PLAGE! POR FAVOR QUE DIRECTION?'

'Bicho?'

'SI PREGO – SORRY PARAGALO – **BEACH BITTE.**'

'No comprende!'

'Oh for goodness sake, you stupid fool, why do you think I'm in swimming shorts carrying this towel and these waterwings? Dear God! Talk about mañanaana. No wonder they lost the war. Imbecilic lot! And they're in the Common Market too. No wonder there's a bloomin' oil lake.'

'Ah. Now I understand you, señor. This is Madrid, our – 'ow do you say – capital city. The nearest sea is five hundred kilometres that way. And, by the way, we were neutral in the war. Who is now the – what was your word – imbecile?'

5 Have proper notes. Frequently, a lecturer will shuffle a pile of papers importantly before launching off on a 50-minute monologue without ever referring to them again. There are three main reasons for having a good set of notes. Firstly, it looks much more professional if you can do a bit of paper shuffling. A pair of reading specs helps to enhance your venerability, particularly if these are half-moon and balanced on your nose so you look over the tops at the audience. Secondly, the notes are there in front of you so that, in the event of an attack of amnesia, you have something for reference. Finally, having slogged away at the subject, to make the notes, you will now have at least a rough working knowledge of what you are going to say – always useful when lecturing. A man who can start speaking without having had the slightest idea of what he is going to say before he opens his mouth is either brave or stupid. Politicians do this a lot, but as everyone expects them to churn out a succession of lies, half-truths and empty promises, what they actually say doesn't really matter.

There are occasions when one can read a written paper or lecture. If you do this, you must read it through, out loud, in private several times before delivery. You must also contrive to have a podium or lectern that is high enough for you to keep one eye on the audience all the time you read – but not so high as to hide you from them. Eye contact is all important.

Many professional comedians will tell you that the secret of comic success is in timing. Lecturing is much the same. When you've just delivered what you are sure was your best and most hilarious joke, give them time to laugh. If, after several seconds, there are no laughs but an embarrassed fidgeting, push on fast. If, in the midst of a mystified silence, one member of the audience is collapsing in hysterics, it will be because her neighbour has just sat on a lime cream and therefore nothing to do with you at all. Timing your exit is pretty important too. If sleeves are being rolled up, you know it's time to take your leave.

Knowing what to wear is vital too, particularly if you are going into this lecturing business to improve your public image as a garden expert. A dark grey or navy suit is out of the question. It would make you look too much like a smooth operator or a city gent. At the other extreme, unless you are a TP, too much of an 'ooh-aah-me-old-pal-me-old-beauty' style could make you look something of a pillock. Your safest bet is to aim for the middle road: Norfolk jacket, twill trousers (no need to tie string round the legs as this is an indoor function), tweedy heather-mixture tie and brown brogues. If you are a man, this sort of outfit will suit almost as well but it is essential to wear a buttonhole. As you now know, TPs usually wear unidentifiable rarities in their buttonholes to score points over their friends. You need not concern yourself with this and can settle for an ordinary rose or carnation, or a leek if you happen to be nationalistic.

For extreme rural venues like village halls you can be a little less formal but be sure to wear thermal underwear – the heating systems could be as primitive as the inhabitants. If you are a man preparing to address an all-woman audience you must be sure this underwear is clean and wholesome. You never know when you might have to have your trousers removed – spillage of coffee, street accident or whatever – you never know.

Subject Matter

While it is perhaps helpful to use a different plot from time to time when novel writing, it is perfectly legitimate to go on delivering the same gardening lecture for year after year without making any conscious effort to change it. With a little scope and imagination, your standard piece could condense to twenty minutes – for Rotary lunch engagements – or extend to an hour for full-scale lectures. You should also be able to make it fit any nominal title from 'A History of the Great Plant Hunters' to 'How to Prepare Dahlias for Exhibition'. To do this you need a master plan. A kind of blueprint to which you can tack extra bits to suit the needs of the evening. The lecture thus falls into an overall shape along these lines:

1 Introduction. Joke – chat about history of plants in general.

2 Main theme. Your personal philosophy about your chosen subject. Hard facts. Soft theories.

3 Controversy time. By now, some of the audience will be asleep, so you'll need to introduce a piece of startling material.

4 Wind up and ask for questions.

This all fits in to my own standard lecture rather like this:

1 The joke: 'Hello. Did you hear the one about the kung fu artist and the contortionist?', or 'Could somebody point out the emergency exits please.' (**History:** see Chapter 9.)

2 Philosophy: My ideas and inclinations are by no means universal but anyone whose tastes differ from mine is a wally. For example, 'I hate dahlias. They're garish, hungry, susceptible to wind, difficult to keep and make perfect havens for earwigs which I hate even more.' (Note: if lecturing to a dahlia society substitute the word *rhododendron* for *dahlia* throughout.) 'I adore gallica roses even though they only flower for a fortnight, get riddled with mildew and make very untidy bushes.' One just rattles on in this vein – the more bigoted you are, the more they say your style is 'inimitable', which you can rate as a compliment.

Hard facts: At this point you'll need to add a bit of solidity by throwing in some good, solid statistics – e.g., 'If every garden centre was laid end to end the sum of their rare and interesting plants would be nearly enough to fill a garden plot one foot by three feet. The only place you can garden with any degree of success in the British Isles is half-way down a Cornish valley on soil with a pH of 2.4.'

Soft theory: Another platform for a bit more of your philosophy.

3 Controversy: Put forward any proposal that sounds preposterous. The more outrageous the better: 'Parliament should pass a bill preventing women from being prime ministers – ' Oh, well. On second thoughts . . . 'The Tate Gallery commissions great and immortal works of art', or 'Unemployment is falling so rapidly that a manpower shortage is forecast for 1990' – anything like that. You can even use horticultural controversy – 'The National Trust has been to gardens what Goebbels was to racial harmony', or 'Kew Gardens is a botanical desert' – anything that will wake 'em up.

4 Get your running shoes on.

The alternative to all this is to prepare a proper talk for each engagement, taking special care to cover the subject mentioned in the title to your best ability. This is a lot more trouble and could be less rewarding and less entertaining for the audience. That is clearly why so few speakers work this way.

Subjects for lectures are not usually very varied. There are several basic types, depending on the tastes of the organisation involved. Most women's associations like to stick to flowers and flower-arranging topics. Unusual plants always stir up plenty of interest and anything unnatural-looking enough to figure in an exhibition flower arrangement will cause tremendous excitement. Horticulture clubs are usually fairly catholic in their tastes and give you a reasonably free rein on subject matter. Men are more likely to be showing vegetables than women – no, no, I don't mean they'll be *showing* women – but in these days of sexual equality it pays to keep an open mind in all things.

The Actual Event

The mechanics of lecturing vary enormously from place to place. Several rules apply. You can always rely on the organisers overestimating audience size. If you are told to expect 100, there will never be more than about 80. Unless you've been before, you will have no idea about the dimensions of the lecture room, the quality of the audience or how useful the facilities are. It pays, therefore, to arrive early.

Say the engagement is for eight o'clock. Be there by half past seven at the latest. You can then unload all your equipment from the car and case the joint for power points, escape routes, where to mount your screen, etc. The first people to arrive are a couple of committee members and a little old lady in an amazingly florid hat topped with fruit and a dead bird. The hat goes quietly to a chair in the back row and falls asleep until the end of the evening. The committee members will eye you furtively and eventually approach you to say:

'Are you Mr Coulton?'

'Colborn. How do you do.' The usual hand pumping follows with embarrassed inanities like, 'Nice now, isn't it. Bit frosty though. Did you get a frost last week – Tuesday?'

'Not Tuesday. Wednesday. I remember 'cause it was darts night.'

'Oh where do you play darts?'

'Here at the club. Is that your screen?'

'Yes. Is that all right there like that?'

'Fine. Fine . . . but.'

'But?'

'We usually like to face away from the stage. Nobody ever talks on the stage. We usually set up our table at the back of the hall and the members all turn their chairs round to face it. More democratic you see.'

It only takes a short time to rearrange all your paraphernalia but you discover that the nearest power point for your slide projector is now about 50 feet away and your wire won't reach. By the time you have sorted out these little technical problems, the audience has gradually filtered in and you can move on to your next most important job (and the reason why you came in so early) – audience assessment. If you are able to disguise the fact that you are the speaker, so much the better. What you have to do is mingle. Keep your ears open and try to gauge the level of their knowledge and enthusiasm. If the talk is erudite, let's hope you've done your homework reasonably well.

'Is Rosemary coming tonight?'

'Neah. She's plant hunting in the Pyrenees. Gorn with the AGS group.'

'Oh, what a pity. I wanted to find out about those tetraploid oreganums. By the way, I've taken your black pansy to Wisley and they have identified it as "Mollie Sanderson".'

'Eah! Clever of them, that. It's a new seedling of mine. I haven't named it yet. "Mollie Sanderson" isn't even a parent.' If the talk is anything like that, you'll need to be very astute.

If, however, it runs something like this:

'Wotcher Ted. The bar's open. Shall we pack a couple in before the shindig starts?'

'Jack! Thought you'd never show. No need to go to the bar, there's a pint for you on the piano. Yours is in the straight glass.'

'What's tonight's geezer like. Is 'e here yet?'

'Bin 'ere half an hour. Hope 'es 'ad previous winding up. I want to get off by nine.'

If the majority of members are like this, you'll have a smooth run as long as you keep it short, feed in plenty of jokes – a bit of actress and bishop routine won't come amiss – and don't go too scientific.

Most horticulture clubs have to wade through their monthly meeting before handing the floor over to the lecturer. This can be staggeringly boring but it is essential that you look attentive and sympathetic while the committee deliberate about whether they can afford the annual trip to Chelsea, whether train or bus is cheaper, whether Harrogate or Southport wouldn't be a better bet, and so on. Eventually the floor is yours – often when you least expect it to be. The most likely occurrence is that after an interminable discussion covering aspects of the last show when somebody broke one of the show cases and didn't own up, the chairman suddenly winds it up by saying: 'Well, time's getting on. If there's no other business Mr Coltbone will now show us a few slides.' Before you can open your mouth, an earnest woman has made a rugby tackle dive for the light switches and the entire room is plunged into Stygian blackness. Silence.

'Er. Could we have the lights on, just for a moment?' you plead. But nobody can see where the switches are now and five or six helpful types are falling over each other and the screen to get the lights on. Worse than the light problem is the fact that your audience haven't a clue who or what you are. This is the direct result of not training your chairman to carry out his proper function and introduce you. Two sentences from him would have made it all so much easier. Mind you, it can make matters worse if he or she gets the facts wrong. You cannot therefore rely on just a verbal briefing. Make sure you have an abbreviated biography – just a couple of lines will do nicely – to push under his nose at the appropriate time. Failure to do this, if you get introduced at all, can result in dangerous misunderstandings.

'Ladies and gentlemen, I'd now like to introduce Mr Lockborn. Mr Lockborn was educated at Kew and ran ICI for seven years before starting his own garden centre in Gloucestershire. His talk tonight will cover all aspects of houseplants. So, without further ado, it gives me pleasure to hand over the floor. Mr Coltorn.' But what *you* told him was that your knowledge of plants was self-taught and that visiting great gardens like Kew had helped in this respect. That you had worked for a small, family business which was later taken over by Mega-Oil and that you had spent a decade developing a new garden at your home and were now selling a few plants to interested garden visitors.

While you are being introduced, your stage fright will be at its peak. As soon as you have started talking, however, it will evaporate and the only precaution you need now take is to keep one eye firmly on the clock. You should know precisely how long to go on and when to stop. This is extremely important. If you feel especially sadistic towards your audience, don't tell them how long the talk will be. Let the poor things fidget and wonder, after half and hour, whether it'll be another five, ten or twenty minutes. You can even shape the lecture so that it comes to an end suddenly, in a couple of phrases, just to heighten the tension.

Illustrations

Some speakers rely entirely on having slides to show. They keep the talk down to the minimum and get the lights out as soon as they can. This is rather a shame and can make for a second-rate performance. Of course, as you are anxious to develop your image as a gardening expert, you will need to spend quite some time talking to your listeners, eyeball to eyeball, with the lights on. Nevertheless, good illustrations are very important and you will have to build up a comprehensive collection of colour slides.

If it existed, reliable equipment would be a useful attribute for the professional lecturer. Sadly, no visual aid equipment ever works. Projectors are the worst. They jam, they refuse to focus, they suddenly run sequences backwards and, worst of all, the bulb can fuse. Inevitably, however carefully you load the slide magazine, one or two will turn out to be upside down or sideways. The only time the slide is the wrong way round is when a sign or notice figures in the picture so that the know-all at the back can spot the mirror writing and shout 'wrong way round!'. The slide that goes onto the screen upside down is always your best shot, or a picture that you wanted to have a particular impact on the audience. By the time it's been flashed on the screen upside down, sideways, upside down again and finally right way up, you have lost the spontaneity and, anyway, everyone is giggling.

Screens, so simple yet so treacherous, can land you in a great deal of trouble and pain. Their main function in life is to trap fingers, but they can also damage people and property in other ways. Table-top models can wreck a good veneer in no time at all and their disconcerting knack of suddenly rolling up with a sound like an explosion can cause heart attacks. My screen used to have a habit of closing itself with imperceptible slowness. Millimetre by millimetre, the top would creep downwards so that, after about 50 slides, the tops of the pictures were just beginning to disappear above the screen. One day, at a WI talk, a very observant lady noticed this trait. After about twenty minutes, the screen had crept to the top of the slide's edge and I calculated that I had plenty of time to get to the end of the batch before carrying out the very ticklish operation of adjusting the frame. However, she leapt from her place and grabbed the screen support at the back. It was too late to do anything, the screen exploded into what looked like a cross between a telescope and an outsize coathanger and fell off the table. The woman's little finger was neatly caught in the folded frame. In my haste to intercept her, I trod on the power line and shot the plug out of the wall – or, more accurately, the wires out of the plug. Darkness.

If your equipment fails completely, you'd better have mugged up on a few funny stories. Your presentation will have been quite ruined and it is no use trying valiantly to proceed with your slide commentary to a blank screen. 'My next slide would have shown Stourhead from the end of the lake. To the right of the picture you would have seen the church in the background and magnolia . . . '. You see, it won't work. So, you've got to change it to, 'A funny thing happened to me on the way to Stourhead, etc.'. Actually, a funny thing *did* happen to me at Stourhead once when I spotted a friend I hadn't seen for over a year carrying a ladder through the bushes.

'Hello,' I said. 'What are you up to?'

'Well you see,' she said, 'we live very close.' I still don't quite know what the encounter was all about because, without a further word of explanation, she plunged back into the bushes, ladder and all. Another year lapsed before I saw her again!

Slides are pleasant for most audiences because they have to be shown in the dark which helps the audience to sleep without being spotted. If this worries you, and you think they should be paying attention, slip in the odd slide that is irrelevant. Even shocking. A 'page three girl' in the middle of a lecture on growing vegetables for showing can work wonders, for example. For mixed audiences with brains, one can be a little more subtle. When demonstrating the way exotic plants fit into English landscapes, I show a herd of zebra grazing in the pastures of Longleat. If there's no reaction, the chances are they're all asleep.

Practical demonstrations, examples and handouts are also useful. Bringing plants along for identification can be great fun. You hand a specimen to the woman on the end of the front row. It gets passed round the entire room during your talk. At the appropriate moment you invite an identity. A couple of people get the wrong plant family, no one else opens his mouth. You now have two choices. You can say, 'I have no idea what it is either,' and hope for an exasperated laugh, or you can say 'it's, for example, *Aquilegia* "Hensol Harebell".' A voluble chorus of disagreement then erupts on all sides, proving, yet again, that plant freaks are ever ready to tell you what a plant isn't, but not what it is.

Question Time

People ask questions at lectures for various reasons. They may quite genuinely want to know the answers. More usually, they want a chance to air their views. Sometimes they may even want to do you down – especially if you are a rival. Here's a typical question-time scenario. You have just given a lecture about using colour schemes in garden planning with illustrations from Gertrude Jekyll, Vita Sackville-West and other historical figures. It was a tricky subject and you spent about fifteen manhours preparing your presentation. The audience consists of about 150 well-to-do people who have come mainly for the madly expensive charity lunch, but partly to hear you. Now, as they say, read on:

Chairman: Now, my lords, ladies and gentlemen, Mr Coblin will be pleased to answer any questions you may have [*resounding silence*] I'm sure someone . . . yes, madam.

Large woman with strawberry-shaped hat: Could you tell us a little about how to grow dahlias?

Speaker: Are you sure you *want* to grow dahlias? [*laughter*] I'd be glad, unless anyone else here is keen, to discuss it with you afterwards.

Hatchet-faced woman in tweed skirt: What's wrong with dahlias?

Speaker: Oh nothing. They're useful in so many ways. I just wondered if anyone would like to ask any questions on the subject we have just been hearing about? Yes sir?

Little man at back: Why do you pronounce Jeckle Jeekill?

Speaker: I don't know. I thought everybody did.

Little man: Well I don't.

Speaker: Jeckle, Jeekill, the pronunciation is, perhaps, less important than her historic contribution to gardening as we know it.

Little man: Are you suggesting that my question is trivial?

Speaker: Not in the least.

Little man: Well, etymology is a hobby of mine. I mean, you don't talk about Dr Jeekill and Mr Hyde do you?

Speaker: No sir, point taken. Anyway, nobody ever gets my name right either. Any other questions?

Chairman: I think, if we could have just one more question on the subject of today's talk, please?

Person in hair shirt and open-toed sandals: When you mentioned places like Sissinghurst and Hidcote, did you realise that toxic pesticides have been used in over 90 per cent of gardens open to the public?

Speaker: No sir, I didn't. I think pesticides are useful to modern gardeners [*sharp intakes of breath from several parts of the hall*] but then, I also sympathise with the philosophy of ecologically minded people and deplore the abuse of chemical sprays.

Sandals: Are you not concerned that multinational chemical firms, mainly stemming from South Africa and other evil régimes, like Washington, apartheid and DDT, are destroying the planet, and that the disappearance of the Cornish language is indicative of the state of things to come?

Chairman: Ladies and gentlemen, I think we have time for what must be the very last question, if someone has one on tonight's subject. I really must ask you to stick to that. Yes madam?

Strawberry-hat woman: I'm still waiting to be told about the dahlias.

Chairman: No, I'm sorry. We must stick to the subject. Yes sir?

Tall military type: Could Mr Coldbain tell us a little about using colour schemes in garden planning – perhaps he could mention a few examples? Gertrude Jekyll. That sort of thing.

Question time at the end of the lecture can be fraught with difficulties, but, to be a good speaker, you will also need to know how to deal with hecklers, mutterers and whisperers. Whisperers are not too bad if they are right at the back but can be very distracting elsewhere in the audience. There are several ways of supressing them. If they are near enough to the front, you can try to overhear what they are saying. If you manage to pick up a phrase or two, use it against them.

'So, ladies and gentlemen, John Claudius Loudon built himself a house at Porchester Terrace, Bayswater and married Jane Wells who became a well-known and respected gardening writer in her own right. Rather like the person you mentioned to your neighbour just now, madam. Oh, sorry! Weren't we supposed to hear? I do beg your pardon, I thought you were making a contribution. Well, to continue . . .'

Open heckling is rare. If it happens to excess, you just have to hope the chairman will throw the troublemaker out. Muttering is quite a different matter. It usually happens in the most knowledge-able circles where it is almost impossible not to spark off a controversy about something or other. This is where you may have to start qualifying your rhetoric with a sprinkling of 'arguably', 'up to a point' and 'possibly'. Talking with a single mutterer is bad enough but, without control, the disease spreads and soon you can have the whole front row at it. One method of suppression is to try to draw the mutterer into the open. You press bravely on thus:

' . . . and, of course, Loudon continued his improvements at Great Tew –'

'Improvements!'

'– where he farmed for several years. His beautification of farm cottages was considered by many to be the beginning of a new age –'

'He must be joking.'

'– when dwelling houses, even of the humble employees, could be enhanced decoratively –'

'No way! Decorative my foot!'

'– for the good of all. Years later, after he had lost his right arm –'

'Wrong arm!'

'– he returned to Great Tew and was pleased with the results of his earlier efforts. Sadly, he was unable to make anything but the crudest of sketches with his left hand but –'

'Wrong again. Loudon never made sketches.'

'– his wife, Jane, wrote copious notes for him. Do you agree with me so far, madam in the front row with the green dress?'

'Absolutely, Mr Coalbread. Do go on!'

Such people are anxious to air their knowledge, but too timid to stand up and be counted. Similar types go in for non-verbal dissent. To every sentence or every concept you issue, they shake their heads vigorously, sometimes groaning slightly or tutting, but never coming forward with a straight question, not even at the end. They are the same people who, at a restaurant, complain bitterly to each other about how disgusting the food is, how the rolls are stale, the steak overdone and the wine acid. When the head waiter approaches to say, 'Everything all right sir? madam?' they always reply, 'Yes, fine thank you.'

Fees

As we discussed earlier, there is no point in lecturing if you are not going to ask for a fee. It's unprofessional to do so. Oddly enough, in a society which seems to get its kicks from fostering envy, we Brits are frightfully reticent when it comes to asking for money. There is something not quite nice about bargaining or negotiating a fee. To ask for more than you are offered is considered very distasteful and, indeed, any conversation on the subject of something as necessary, but thoroughly undesirable, as money is likely to be stilted and uneasy.

'What is your motivation in all this?' I was once asked during an exercise in journalism.

'I'm doing it for the money,' I replied.

'Oh, I see,' was the answer, 'a sort of prostitution.'

I suppose there are considerable parallels between the oldest profession and public entertainment. Both provide a service and in both there is an element of pleasure – those that enjoy doing it most are usually best at it . . . er, so I'm told. But when it comes to money, many of our greatest experts find it deeply embarrassing. This is something you will need to overcome. Just like your natural inhibitions, which you banished by talking gibberish at the mirror, your reserve about money must go too. If it doesn't, you soon won't have enough in reserve!

One way to start is to bargain with everybody. Try it with a London cabby – they can be awfully helpful. On arrival at your destination, when he says, 'Two seventy-five please, squire,' try him out by saying: 'How about two quid straight?' He'll respect you for your commercial pluck. You should also make sure you always get a few per cent off all purchases. Wherever you shop, ask for a discount. Usually you'll collect abuse but occasionally you'll score and save twopence. Getting estimates will also help you to develop your trading acumen. Professionals are the very worst at assuming you will pay whatever fee they think appropriate. Take the average surgeon for example. If he tells you your hernia operation will sting you £500 plus possible hospital extras, why not tell him you want it done for £400?

You could say, 'Right, doc – sorry, mister – here's a hundred up front, right? Now you fix the operation for Friday week and if it's successful, I'll lob you another three in cash. No questions asked. Whaddya say?' You see how simple it is? All you need is the *guts* to do it.

Commanding the right fee for lecturing is just the same in reverse. It's best to negotiate it before the event but, occasionally, this isn't practicable. So, at the end of the evening when you are about to take your leave the treasurer creeps up, cheque book in hand and says, 'Just before you go, can we discuss your um, gulp, fee?'

'Certainly,' you say, and here comes the crafty bit. You do not mention a figure at all – if you do, he'll know that is your maximum expectation and he'll know you're willing to move down from there. 'What had you in mind?'

'Er, well, I'm sure I don't know um . . . er . . . twenty-five?' And you still say absolutely nothing. Look at the floor, look at him but keep silent. You now know his minimum. He goes on to say,

'Well, er what about thirty-five?' A very long pause, and then:

'Well . . . I have lectured for as little as that, but not for many many years.'

'I'm afraid the committee have not empowered me to write a cheque for more than fifty without a special meeting.' You know that is his limit, so go for it.

'Well, you're a lovely bunch of characters. It's been a delightful audience. I'll go for that little just this once.'

'You'll accept fifty?'

'Absolutely. You can make the cheque out to me personally for fifty-seven fifty.'

'But you said you'd accept fifty.'

'That's right. The other is VAT.'

You will find, at the beginning of your career as a public speaker, that most of your engagements take place on the coldest nights of the year, in the dreariest of village halls and to the smallest of audiences. Frequently the committee of a gardening club will outnumber the audience. Often, meetings will be cancelled because of weather or abandoned through lack of support. However, don't get depressed about all this. Remember, it is your first positive step to fame. In future years, when thrilling letters marked BBC come in the post and you become a national media personality, you'll look back on those village hall days with regret and nostalgia. And think of the appearance fees you'll be able to charge then! Only £500 to drive off to some bash, climb out of your car, make a short speech declaring this garden centre open or that foundation laid, pocket your cheque and drive off to the five-star pub they've booked for you. The only difficulty is that by the time you've moved this far along in your career, you'll be so busy collecting appearance fees, you won't have any time left for serious gardening.

Chapter 8

Building a Collection

'Human acquisitiveness is a major hazard to plants.'

(Brickell & Sharman, *The Vanishing Garden*,
John Murray, 1986)

The horticultural world is split in two. There will come a point, as
your expertise progresses, when you must decide which camp to
join. On the one hand there are people who call themselves
'gardeners'. This is the larger of the two groups and comprises
more or less any expert who is potty about plants of most kinds
and sees a garden as somewhere where they can be enjoyed in
pleasant surroundings. The second group is made up of people
who regard themselves as landscape architects. They see gardens
as extensions of buildings and think plants should play second
fiddle to their architectural prowess.

The trouble with architecture is that it offers the perpetrator a
wider opportunity to offend the sensibilities of more people than
any other art form. People only see paintings or listen to music
of their choice. If you dislike Bacon or Stockhausen, you can
keep away. But what about Centre Point, Guildford Cathedral
or the new Lloyd's building? There they are, dominating their
surroundings so that passers-by have no choice but to cringe in
their shadows. William Robinson, a famous Edwardian gardener,
was strongly in favour of keeping architects out of gardens. He
wrote:

> Architects as such have no knowledge of our garden
> flora, and for ages gardens were disfigured owing to their
> endeavours to conform trees to the lines of buildings. (*The
> English Flower Garden* 1883, 1934 edition.)

A 'landscaper' will use man-made structures to excess. His garden will be punctuated by stone stairways, rustic arches, pillars supporting cross-members draped with wisteria, pleached-tree walks and, inevitably, rank upon rank of yews clipped into anything so long as it doesn't resemble a tree. There are yew galleons, peacocks, obelisks, arches, cubes and balls. Plants will be placed strictly according to colour, shape and 'texture' – landscapers talk a good deal about texture – and will be planted within the confines of these artificial structures. There are even places where plants disappear completely. Japanese gardens of rocks and raked gravel are beginning to appear in parts of Britain nowadays and are loudly applauded by the landscapers.

In the early days of the century, when labour was cheap and good materials two a penny, it was possible to create some quite pleasing examples of garden architecture. Plants soon grew up and softened the hard edges, diminishing the prominence of the stonework and producing an attractive air of decay. Nowadays, when the only materials easily available are modern imitations of old natural stone or harsh new bricks, there is a danger that the 'architected' garden will disappear under a heap of neatly pointed concrete. Just look at some of the Chelsea Flower Show gardens these days. 'Natural' streams have become brick-sided chasms, areas of yard known as 'patios' are paved with slabs more suitable for shopping precincts, and planting, though admittedly not in neat rows, looks about as natural as an oil refinery. You can imagine some of the different theme gardens we'll probably see there next year:

A Cottage Garden   *For your dreamy retreat in rural Cockfosters. Concrete slabs surrounded by flower beds containing all the old favourite cottage perennials – Sweet Williams, marigolds, foxgloves, rhododendrons, azaleas and hostas.*

A Town Garden   *For that chic little £900,000 terraced cupboard in Kensington. Elegantly laid concrete slabs surrounded by Vogue-style flowers chosen for scent and class – Solomon's seal, paeonies, lilies, rhododendrons, azaleas and hostas.*

A Wildlife Garden   *For the family who cares about butterflies and wild beasties. Informally laid concrete slabs surrounded by nettles, meadow cranesbill, violets, cowslips, rhododendrons, azaleas and hostas.*

A Limestone Garden *For gardeners on chalky or limy soil who can't grow lime-haters. Ground completely paved over with concrete slabs. Several large containers filled with lime-free compost and planted with rhododendrons, azaleas and hostas.*

A Water Garden *A series of raised structures, surfaced with concrete slabs and containing, at different levels, a series of little ponds that overflow into each other ceaselessly. Planted with water plants but surrounded with raised beds of rhododendrons, azaleas and hostas.*

A Rock Garden *A big rockery for the large garden. Huge lumps of Alp crowd in on a mountain torrent whose banks are planted with rhododendrons, azaleas and hostas.*

If the thought of all this structural rigidity sets your teeth on edge, the chances are you'll be joining the 'gardener' camp. But, to be a good gardener, you'll still need a lot of artistic flair for layout and design, even if you don't go to the extremes of the purist landscape types. Most TPs are in this category, of course, but you don't have to be a good plantsman to deplore artificiality. On the other hand, plants are the gardener's raw material and if he has a wide range of them his garden is more likely to be a success. Thus, to be a well-grounded expert, you will need to build up a good collection of interesting plants. If you want to keep one step ahead of your rivals, many of these will have to be rare as well.

People build up their collections in different ways. There are few gardeners who can say, with a clear conscience, that they have never snitched so much as a cutting or a few seeds. Everyone who travels abroad knows that sponge bags are essential equipment for shipping home plant material and are so much more discreet than Wardian cases (see Chapter 2). However, there are those who carry plant stealing beyond this minor pinching into the realms of serious larceny. One of our most famous English gardens was allegedly stocked with loot swiped over a lifetime from friends, rivals, national institutions – anywhere the owner could operate without fear of retribution. His style was impressive – it seemed the more obvious and daring he was, the more he got away with – literally! Even when he was visiting gardens with a group, he would hang back from the main body to fill his pockets with whatever he fancied.

For dedicated kleptomaniacs, certain items of equipment are essential. In public gardens it helps to have a large badge readable from quite a distance, that says 'SEED COLLECTOR'. Wearing one of those enables you to browse away to your heart's content, not only taking as much seed as you like, but also lifting cuttings, bulbils, seedlings from under parent plants – whatever you need. You could actually ask the security guard or attendant to show you where different species are growing without attracting suspicion. You will also need bags and envelopes for your booty, but need not conceal these at all because you will be doing everything quite openly. Mind you, I wouldn't recommend you to continue your activities in the gift shop. Swiping seeds in an official capacity is one thing. Pocketing tea towels, pot pourri kits and lavender bags is quite another and there is a good chance you will be arrested and charged.

Without a seed collector's badge, you will have to resort to stealth. You will need to carry a number of polythene bags, have a coat with deep pockets, or carry an umbrella which is closed but unclipped so that you can drop cuttings into it. If it begins to rain, whatever you do, don't open your umbrella. The embarrassment of standing under a sudden rain of plant shoots has to be experienced to be believed. You will also need a sharp knife – the small, red Swiss army types are good because they stay sharp and the more expensive versions have tiny 3-inch saws for woody cuttings. Carting loppers round a garden is likely to arouse suspicion and, although secateurs will fit into large pockets, it isn't half painful when you forget they're there and sit on them in the tea room.

'Good afternoon sir, would you like to sit here?'

'Thank you. May I have a pot of tea, please, and some of those delicious-looking AAAARGH!!!'

You should also carry labels with you so that, when you get home, you'll know what you've stolen. Another popular and widely used alternative is to steal the labels from the plants in the public garden – in fact, there are those who take the whole thing to its logical conclusion and remove plant, label and a good pocketful of soil as well, leaving a neat little hole behind them for other visitors to enjoy.

Another form of kleptomania, and no less reprehensible, is to be found among so-called wild flower enthusiasts. These people, armed with trowel and basket, stop at the roadside or enter other people's woods to collect for themselves large quantities of primroses, cowslips or whatever else they feel like having. These are then transported home and planted in unsuitable positions in their gardens where they usually die. It is a disgraceful thing to do and should be stamped out at once! Luckily, there are quite heavy fines nowadays for people caught ransacking the hedgerows and quite right too! The morality of this practice is clearly quite dreadful. Those wild plants belong to the landowners and are their responsibility. They are there to be sprayed by farmers, cut back by council verge mowers or sacrificed for development – not to be filched by amateur naturalists. So leave your trowel at home and leave ecological destruction to the professionals. Got it? Right!

If you shrink from the thought of stealing from gardens – and I hope you do – actually I'm quite surprised you'd even thought of it as a way to acquire a collection – an enjoyable, legal, and more or less moral way of finding sources of plants is to join some of the specialist societies. There are plenty of them and most have close ties with the Royal Horticultural Society. (No serious gardener can possibly afford not to belong to the RHS.) There's no shortage of choice, it depends what turns you on, as they say. There's the Lily Group, for instance – not, as you might think, a gaggle of poets who want to revive Pre-Raphaelite painting and stand about wearing velvet suits holding lilies, but rather an erudite lot who get together from time to time to exhibit their finest specimens. Watching the members in action can be awe inspiring; erectness, length of stem and shape of bloom are all important. The Alpine Garden Society is a bit more general in its tastes – they enthuse over anything 6 inches or shorter. There are dozens of other groups and part of the fun will be for you to decide which ones to join. Choosing doesn't have an awful lot to do with the types of plants, but with the people in the groups. Certain species attract certain types and if your face doesn't fit, change your speciality or expect to be cast as a misfit. It is dangerous to generalise, of course, but here are a few examples of society plants.

Camellias Associated with the finest gardens. If you are not entitled to wear a coronet and don't work for the National Trust, perhaps you should consider a different group.

Saxifrages Dedicated saxifrage devotees have much in common with the whippet and canary breeders of the old industrial north. If you play in your local brass band and enjoy whelks or saveloys, the chances are you're a saxifrage man.

Roses Two camps here. Nasty modern and posh old. Modern shrub roses that need no pruning are posher than floribundas. Patio and ground cover roses are unspeakable – getting the idea? One more thing. Growing roses for showing has nothing whatever to do with gardening – it is a pure ritual based on ancient pagan rites, where little bags are tied all over the rose bushes to make the garden look as horrible as possible.

Chrysanthemums Strictly for the funereal type. If the very scent of their leaves gives you goose bumps down the back and makes you think of harvest thanksgiving with fond nostalgia – join the group. If they set you counting the number of funerals you've been to recently and balancing these off against weddings and christenings – forget chrysanthemums.

Variegated plans (Very *'Homes and Gardens'*). Some people get quite obsessive about plants with pus-coloured streaks on their leaves. The occasional variegated evergreen is all right up to a point, but these people fill every cranny with anything that manifests a pigment disorder. A new freak, such as a primrose with green and white leaves, or a golden choisya will send them into raptures.

Large tree societies (see camellias). After the 1987 October hurricane there are more members than trees.

Fuchsias If you haven't got the message about fuchsias by now, you are clearly eligible to join a fuchsia society. Be warned, they take exhibiting very seriously indeed and expect a high level of cultural ability. Make sure you know all the good exhibition varieties.

Auriculas As long as you don't expect any of the show varieties to perform outside, and provided you like flowers that are not only basically green, black and brown but are also covered with a dust-coloured meal, this is the group for you. Be prepared to know about vine weevil.

Specialist groups have great fun staging exhibits at shows,

swapping seeds and plants and organising trips. If you decide to be an active member and help with these functions, make sure you are flush with spare time and mind they don't take too much advantage of you. Volunteer to supply a plant for a show stand and you could find you have the whole exhibit to stage. You need to watch out for the purists too. They can be very intense and rather frightening. It is said that fights have broken out over the naming of certain varieties. This may be exaggerating but there is no doubt that feuds have run on for generations. The secret with these specialist groups is to ease your way in gently, taking great care to avoid treading on anyone's corms. (It's a joke, not a misprint.)

Two members, female, of the National Conserving Club for Phantom Gardeners arrive at a show carrying some monkshood.

'Hullo, Susan. Are we the first in the hall? Where is our pitch?'

'Right near the side exit, Nancy. Same as last year.'

'Let's hope it isn't the fiasco it was last year. Who's helping this time?'

'Sebastian, Dr Gleet, the usual crowd.'

'Sebastian Hermitage? He's useless. Doesn't know an alstro-emeria from a french bean.'

'I know, but he is a botanist. They like to be involved.'

'Well, you'll have to keep him and Dr Gleet apart. They'll be squabbling all the time otherwise. Hullo, who's this coming over?'

'NCCPG?' asks the newcomer.

'Indeed we are, for our sins.'

'I'm Cyril Bennlait. A new member. I wondered if there was anything I could do to help?'

'Hooray, join the club! I'm Susan Dredging and this is Nancy Gatehinge. I expect you've seen her book. I say Nancy, you're not putting *that* in the display, are you?'

'Well, yes. Why not?'

'Because Colonel Bloodgood is on the judging committee this year and, well, you know his views on monkshood.'

'I can't help it if his favourite horse ate one once and died of colic. I mean, for heaven's sake, it was thirty years ago. Anyway, I'm going to include it this time so there!'

'It'll cost us our medal.'

'Don't care.'

'Which monkshood are you calling it?' asks Cyril.

'*Carmichaelii*,' says Nancy.

'You can be sure Dr Gleet'll know different. Ah. Here he is.'

'Hullo everyone. Sorry I'm a touch late. Had to deliver a baby.'

'Oh how sweet. What sex?'

'Both,' says Gleet, enigmatically.

'Twins!'

'No, just the one baby.'

'Oh, how very unfortunate,' voices lowered to show suitable sympathy.

'Not really. This baby is a new hybrid pink I've bred. I've delivered it to committee room A to see if they'll give it an award – ha ha ha ha! That had you all guessing for a minute what? what? ha ha ha ha. I say, where's that posing botanist, Huffy Hermitage, I mean?'

'Over there, keep your voice down. Though I have to agree, he's not my cup of tea at all.'

'Neither mine. Not by a long chalk. But botanists are often a pain in the you-know-what. Have you met Cyril Bennfleet, our newest member?'

'Hullo Bennfleet.'

'Bennlait actually. How do you do?'

'I do all right, thanks. Gardening's a lot more fun than doctoring, what? I say, Nancy. I haven't seen that monkshood for years. It's *arendsii* of course.'

'*Carmichaelii* actually.'

'Oh come off it, the colour's wrong. Besides, it's not branched enough.'

'It is *carmichaelii*. My mother left it to me.'

'OK. If you say so. Look, here comes Haughty Hermitage, let's ask 'im. Whatever he calls it we'll go for the opposite, what? what? what? . . . Sebastian! how very nice to see you, what?'

'Morning Gleet, everyone. Hullo Cyril, I'm so glad you could join us. Do you know everyone here – folks, this is my oldest friend and fellow botanist, Cyril –' Once the embarrassment is over, they resume haggling over the monkshood.

'Can't possibly be *napellus*, it's too late.'

'Far too early for *arendsii*. Besides –'

'– *volubile*?'

'Oh don't be ridiculous. Besides, you pronounce it "volubial" – not "voloobilly".'

'But this could be a climber. We can only see the flower, not the whole plant. Anyway, I said "volubeely", not "billy".'

'So why not ask Nancy?'

'Well, Nancy, is it a climber?'

'I've already told you it's *Aconitum carmichaelii*. It's not a climber and it's not anything else.'

'Impossible. That's cream – never blue. Why don't you ask Cyril.'

'Why? Are you a hardy plant man, Cyril?'

'In a manner of speaking.'

'Well. What do you think?'

'Think?'

'Can you identify this plant?'

'Certainly. It's a form of *Aconitum carmichaelii* known as "Arendsii".'

'Well really!'

Do you think you'll be happy wih that lot? If your enthusiasm is waning, just remember that while all the ridiculous discussions go on, those specialist societies are helping to preserve and multiply all kinds of superb plants that you would not otherwise be able to find. It is your duty as a gardener to put up with all this and throw your weight behind the group, not at it.

If you are well off and physically fit, you can go on collecting tours all over the world. Specialist groups and societies organise their own tours but plenty of adventurers go plant collecting on their own. There are three basic types of trip: the look-don't-touch tour where collecting is forbidden; the in-depth-study tour where you might come away with a little seed but where your main object is to learn about the environment of the region you are visiting and to respect its ecology and, finally, there is the full-scale plant collecting trip whose sole object is to acquire new specimens to bring back and introduce into cultivation. Intrepid explorers have been going on plant hunting trips for the last 400 years or so, but new species are still being introduced. Today there is something of a race against time for many of the world's species are vanishing. How sad to have to say that many of these are vanishing because of collecting. Perhaps, unless you know exactly what you are doing, you'd better stick to the look-don't-touch approach.

Your first and most important need for plant tours is lots and lots of money. Many of the look-don't-touch trips are designed for very well-off types who expect a high degree of luxury. Although some will be genuinely interested in what they see, a fair proportion will only be there to swank about it afterwards.

'Darling, I haven't seen you for absolute ages. Where've you been?'

'Nepal, darling.'

'Oh you lucky brute. I'm *dying* to go. How was it?'

'Heaven. We stayed at the most divine little hotel run by a Swiss family. Immaculate. Had its own swimming pool, sauna and lovely views.'

'And those wonderful plants!'

'Gerald went off plant hunting with the tour. I just stayed and lapped up the *ambiance* in the hotel. They served real French coffee and actually made their own croissants. It was so beautifully civilised.'

'What was the local food like?'

'You can't eat the local food darling, it's not safe. Dead goat and things. Yecchh! Gerald had some on the plant tours and got the most frightful squitters. He's lost half a stone. But luckily the Swiss owner supervises the cooking in the hotel so we were all right. Finding the right materials is a bit difficult for them though. I don't think we saw more than one kiwi fruit all the time we were there.'

If your funds are limited, a good place to start getting serious about plants is the Mediterranean. From Gibralter all the thousands of miles round that ocean to North Africa, most of the tourist industry is geared for summer crowds. This means that from November to May there is plenty of spare accommodation for visitors and bargains are to be had. Most north Europeans visit the Med in summer. Millions of them head for that narrow spit of sand between the hideous ribbons of concrete development and the sewage-rich sea. By August, every inch is covered with a tide of sunburnt flesh. Behind the ghastly coastal strips – all looking more or less the same whether it be Spain, Italy or Israel – the coastal hills are brown, sterile and too hot to walk. Look for plants up in the maquis in August and even the silver-foliaged toughies are half dead. The only living things are snakes and lizards. But visit the same spots in spring and you enter a plantsman's paradise. For a start the hills are green. Several different species of lavender will be in flower, with bees and birds active everywhere. Among the tough, wiry stems of the little shrubs you'll find a wealth of delicate bulbs – narcissi in Iberia, cyclamen in Cyprus, wonderful blood-red anemones in Greece, irises in Turkey and so much more. There are rockroses – more than you thought could possibly exist – and they hybridise too. Spiny euphorbias gleam with luminescent flowers the colour of half-ripe lemons, and the number of different wild orchids, especially on the floors of the pine woods, is staggering.

There are plenty of tours organised in the Mediterranean and the secret is to make sure you get in with a group of people you like. The success of these tours depends very much upon the quality of the tour leader. If he or she is rather a wet blanket – as can often happen – your enjoyment can be ruined. Of course, after a few years of travel, as you are intending to be a true garden expert, you will be expected to become a tour leader yourself. The duties of tour leader are many and varied and do not necessarily have a lot to do with plant hunting. You must be a reasonably competent mountaineer, nanny, butler, entertainer, confessor, diplomat, navigator, porter, driver, negotiator and, of course, plant expert.

When you lead your tour you must make absolutely sure you meet certain requirements. First, it helps to know the area your group is exploring. Painful hours spent with maps, compasses and uncomprehending natives won't impress the clients one bit. If you are still lost as night falls, panic may set in and they could round on you in quite an aggressive fashion. Secondly, you should have a reasonable idea of the sort of plants you are likely to find. Most of the people in your group will consider themselves eminent experts and everybody will be trying furiously to score points over each other. However, in any group you will always have one particular know-all and it will be your job to squash him at every opportunity. If you don't, he will squash you. If you are really unlucky he will know all there is to know, not only about the local flora but also about local geology, food, wine, politics and wild animals. Once the group starts looking to him for succour and advice rather than you, you've had it; you'll never be able to discipline them again. You'll recognise him as soon as you see your party assembling at the departure point in the UK. He'll be the one in the Tyrolean hat, lederhosen and hiking boots. Everyone else will be wearing that item of uniform essential to British tourists all over the world – the plastic raincoat.

You get your little party into the bus. The Tyrolean hat sits in the front and while you're shuffling the papers on your clipboard he says, 'I'm Peter Mindbender. I expect you've heard of me.'

'Yes indeed Mr Mindbender. You're on my list. I've heard of all my passengers because they're on my list.'

'That's not what I meant.'

'Actually, you are sitting in Miss Tesco's seat. Yours is on the other side.'

'Oh I'd rather sit here, if you don't mind. I'm familiar with these Leybridge Roadqueen Mark Five buses. This seat has the least motion of any in the passenger section.'

'Well then, perhaps it would be kinder if you let Miss Tesco benefit from that.'

By now you know full well that this specimen is going to be trouble. You'll need to watch him like a hawk. You do your intro speech, running through some of the places they're going to visit – meanwhile, he explains loudly to his neighbour that various different routes would be much better, that there would be more to see if you had chosen a Roadqueen Mark Six with the redesigned window frames and vista roof, that the party should have bought their drachmas before leaving and so on. When you get on the ferry, everyone dashes off to their cabins and an hour or two later you wonder whether it's safe to creep into the bar. Miss Tesco leaps at you from behind a pillar.

'Oh *there* you are. We wondered where you'd got to. Everyone's over there.' But you can see that. They're all clustered round one table while a single, already too familiar voice is saying: '. . . stabilisers in rough weather because they'd get damaged so they turn them off and let the boat roll.' One or two faces are already turning a bit green but he presses on. 'Of course, it's a well-known medical fact that sea sickness is based on insecurity. Why, the very thought of this tiny little vessel bobbing about in seven hundred feet of water, miles from land is enough to make people feel ill. And you can never be quite sure what the safety precautions are like – I mean how would everyone fit into those lifeboats? Nobody had time in the *Titanic* anyway, they just froze in the water.'

'I think we should change the subject,' you say, trying to break the spell. But there's no stopping him now, in spite of the greenish pallor of the faces all round him.

'Of course, I always think the best way to cope with sea sickness is to eat a good, hearty meal. Have a good breakfast, I'd say. A big fry-up with plenty of bacon, sausages, fried bread – perhaps a few mushrooms. And at lunch, don't be afraid to have the sweet too – a good rich trifle or Black Forest gâteau, topped with lashings of cream – I say, Miss Tesco, are you feeling all right? 'Straordinary thing. Running out of the room like that. Can't be seasick – the ship's barely rolling. Whose round is it? Mine's a gin and advocaat with extra raw egg.'

When you land at Piraeus – I know they haven't got a ferry that goes from England to Piraeus yet but this is where you'll have to exercise your imagination – he's the one who makes the wrong remark at customs so that instead of waving you all through, they decide to search everyone. But when the order is given to open the suitcases, he is the one who objects. 'I say,' he says to you, 'I do think you ought to lodge a complaint. This really is rather unfair.'

'Well, you did mention that cannabis would grow well in this climate, just as we were going through the green channel.'

'So it would, old boy. What on earth's that got to do with it? Are you sure you're cut out for this tourleading business?'

'No.'

'Well, if you want me to take over at all, just say the word, old boy. I've done this sort of thing dozens of times.'

Eventually, after an interminable journey into the hills, grinding round corners with mountains towering above you on one side and bottomless chasms on the other, you arrive at the inn where you and your group will be staying. On the evening before your first foray into the surrounding hills, you give a little talk, with slides, about the various plants they'll be seeing. Mindbender disagrees with every species you name and queries every location and that's the way it goes, all through the trip.

The second type of trip, where you will do a little modest collection, is best organised on an individual basis. The difficulty about collecting this way is that few plants produce flowers and seeds at the same time. Flowers, for the most part, are showy. As well as being easy to find, we usually identify the plants we find by studying the flowers. Seed capsules are frequently difficult to identify. You may think you are, for instance, collecting seeds of a beautiful and rare wild pea which, on germination, turns out to be some weedy old vetch that grows half a mile away from your back door at home.

The other problem is with customs and regulations. Generally speaking, it is quite a sensible idea to abide by the rules, even if you think some of them are silly. This means contacting the Ministry of Agriculture for information about permits. You should also have a working knowledge of the local rules – if such exist – and, whatever you do, refrain from working against the natural laws of ecology. In plain English, that means don't ransack a habitat by digging up a carload of plant material wherever you go. A small envelope to contain a few seeds is all you need for each plant. So beware. Fines are big these days and imprisonment not off the cards.

A jolly way to do this kind of collecting is to combine it with a holiday. Take nothing more than your car, a passport, seed envelopes and clean knickers. Have a vague overall plan, but be flexible. There are various good reasons for this. If you are going into a large mountain range, the seasons are variable, not only from year to year, but also from alp to alp. One may have a little snow left near the top. Thus, if it is July on the lower slopes, you will still find spring gentians, geums and pasque flowers up near the snow. However, mountains are notoriously fickle and if, after six consecutive days of steady rain – rain, moreover, which is falling as snow twenty minutes' walk up the mountainside – you feel totally brassed off with the whole thing, you can up sticks and drive off to say, central France where it is hot and dry. Finding accommodation is usually the least of your worries.

'*Bonjour, monsieur. Vous êtes Allemands?*'

'*Non, Anglais. Avez-vous quelques personnes ici qui parlent Anglais?*'

'Of course, *monsieur*. Many of our visitors are English.'

'Oh. Have you any English people staying here today?'

'No, *monsieur*.'

'Oh, fine. In that case, may I ask what your room rate is?'

'Certainly, *monsieur*. A double room will cost you sixty francs.'

'I say, that's incredibly cheap.'

'Yes, monsieur.'

'And supper?'

'From one hundred francs, but we have a *menu gastronomique* at two hundred francs. It is *formidable*.'

'It should be for that money. What sort of things do you specialise in?'

'On the *gastronomique?* You start with a clear soup made from the wings of the, 'ow do you say? thrush, then *Moules à la Maison* – that's mussels taken out of the shell, marinaded in seventy-five-year-old armagnac for two days, lightly fried in pure olive oil to which one caraway seed has been added, placed in a small pastry cup that has been baked blind, covered with a special *gelée* extracted from a kind of local seaweed . . .'

'Local seaweed? I thought we were two hundred kilometres from the sea.'

'It is, as you would say, seaweed of the river. Er, to continue, *monsieur*, it is served with half an olive. Then you have *Filet de Merlin Laurent Perrier* – that's, 'ow you call it, whiting flakes with all the bones removed, baked for six hours in a slow cooker with a quarter of a litre of Auvergne goat's milk, a leaf of fennel and one shallot. Then a sorbet flavoured with lemon and the leaves of meadow clary to clary the palate – aha, you must excuse me, *monsieur*, I must 'ave my little joke! Then we have *Entrecôte au Ned Sherrin*, prepared with a rich but not satiating sauce and a little salad of wild dandelion and sorrel. Our *fromages* include fifty-four varieties and for desserts we have the *Fabrication des Fraises de Bois au Geoff Capes* – a *crème Anglais* with wild strawberries served in a special crisp, edible wafer dish and garnished with crystallised rose petals.'

'Oh I say. You have quite overwhelmed me. We'll book one of your double rooms and reserve a couple of places for the gastronomic supper please.'

'*Absolument pas, monsieur*! Do you not realise this is Bastille Day? We are absolutely, 'ow do you say? choc a log!'

'Block.'

'Oh pardon, *monsieur*. Block a log.'

'Can you suggest anywhere near here that might have a room?'

Gallic shrug.

The French countryside is delightful because it is so roomy. There are as many people living in the whole of France as there are of us crammed onto our tiny islands. Bits of French land get left to nature here and there from Normandy to Navarre. Cart tracks, woods, river banks and even canal sides seem to offer so much more to picnicker, butterfly watcher or whatever. What's more, nobody seems to mind if you wander about on their fields. Obviously, you don't trespass by pinching crops or damaging property, but, meet a farmer on his own patch and he will either ignore you or greet you with that careless courtesy the French usually reserve for each other. Once, I was so taken with a field of overripe barley in the Auvergne, I just had to get closer. The golden ears were a perfect match for the red of the poppies and the intense blue of the cornflowers. I even fantasised about recreating such a patch of corn in my garden at home – well, why not? You could sow a mix of cereal and cornfield weed seeds – corn marigold, corn cockle, fluellin, larkspur (only the blue ones of course) and Venus's looking glass. I then noticed that the cornflowers had plenty of ripe seed, so I waded into the crop and filled my pockets. As I was plucking the heads and thrashing out the seed into my hand, the owner strolled past with a chainsaw in his hand. Despite visions of playing a live role in a video nasty, all I collected was a cheery wave – nothing more. None of the English Farmer approach.

'Excuse me. Do you know you're on private property?' Not even a querulous 'Can I help you?' But then, in England, the barley would have been devoid of cornflowers and would have been combined weeks before when it was ready.

Once your idyll comes to an end and you are home, sowing the collected seed needs careful planning. Some may be difficult to germinate so it pays to split your sowing among various treatments. Inevitably, you will produce many more plants than you need but this is where the fun of swapping with fellow enthusiasts comes in. Besides, think of the opportunities for oneupmanship. 'Can I tempt you to a few plants of *Gentiana lutea*. I collected the seed myself, from Monc Blanc last July. Oh, and do let me give you some *Lathyrus*. Such a charming Breton peasant got them for me. We had lunch with them in a tiny village miles from St Malo – you couldn't possibly know it.'

The third type of plant hunting expedition is for real keenies. Usually the costs and administration are immense, so it is necessary for such trips to be sponsored in some way. These expeditions are invariably long and rugged and should only be attempted by people who are physically very fit, psychologically robust and extremely good at getting on with other people. Sharing a camper van or a small tent for eight weeks with someone who has a lot to learn about personal hygiene or has disturbing private habits can be a great drain on one's resources of bonhomie. Tales of adventure from people who have been on trips of this kind make terrifying listening. Not because they've been in intense physical danger, or even at risk from political upheavals – those were vicissitudes they all took comfortably in their strides like the great plant hunters who trod those paths before them. The real horror stories concern the antics of their fellow travellers.

'With a *native* girl?'

'Who said anything about girl?'

'Poor, poor Anthea.'

'Poor Anthea be damned. She was on the trip too.'

'I beg your pardon?'

'Same native. Now you mustn't breathe a word of this to anybody. Nobody else on the expedition really knew. They suspected but they couldn't be sure.'

'But how did you . . . er, which, er plants did you like best?'

'Of course, it was very difficult for me because I was the only unattached female and Miles Parse-Pedant the only unattached male. There was nothing for it but to share his tent.'

'Heavens, did you feel safe? I mean what about at night?'

'What about at night?'

'Well, yes. I mean did anything happen? Any harassment?'

'Absolutely not. Not interested.'

'Well? What was it like?'

'Horrendous! We were limited on water so washing was not something you could do a lot of. Parse-Pedant's feet stayed in the same socks the whole time. He also snored deafeningly and tossed and turned like a soul in torment. He was noisier asleep than awake I think. His nose was barely out of a book. I think he's still one of those Oxford dons who think females are invariably too silly to bother to talk to. He'd have hours of in-depth discussions with Cedric about the effect of cosmic rays on natural hybridisation – actually, he talked a lot of rubbish most of the time – but whenever I identified a genus or species he just looked as though he were having an enema.'

'What *can* you mean?'

'Then there were the breathing exercises.'

'Breathing exercises?'

'Learnt them from a Tibetan monk who was reading business studies at the varsity. Every morning, *before* dawn. The first morning I nearly died of fright. This ghastly death rattle, in the dark, getting louder and more laboured. I thought he was being strangled by bandits. I screamed, lit a candle and there he was. Standing on his head, nothing on except a pair of grimy Y-fronts and, of course, the socks, black in the face doing these awful groans.'

'My God! How frightful!'

'I asked him if he was all right. What did he do? Tore me off a strip for disturbing his meditation. Said I was ruining a creative process. I was to remember that we were living in a confined space for a few weeks and would I kindly show some consideration and blow the candle out.'

'He sounds a treasure. What's he a professor of?'

'Archaeology.'

'Oh well, he'll have been helpful on the ruins, anyway.'

'So we all thought. In fact that's rather why he was asked to join the expedition, but he said it was the wrong area and the wrong period for him. Anway, he told us he spent most of his time at a computer these days. Hadn't done a dig for a quarter of a century – actually boasted that! Still collating the data, or some such bilge. No wonder Oxford's going bust!'

'Isn't he the one that's going to the States next year for a whole year?'

'That's the one. Sabbatical. Quite a junket, I can tell you. Still, it'll mean he misses out on the next expedition. I think I might go again.'

'Imogen, really! What about your house and everything?'

'To hell with the house. Harry's too busy working to see me these days and I want to get back to the hills – there's so much more to find.'

'You're not going to the same place are you?'

'Rather. We've barely scratched the surface. I want to get among those *Meconopsis quintuplinerva* again. You can't imagine the joy of finding them – like super-blue harebells.'

'Will you be employing the same native guide?'

'Rather!'

Such trips are becoming quite the fashion . . . .

But this type of collecting is only for those who can spare the time and the money. The rest of us can have nearly as much fun collecting from gardens and nurseries at home. There are so many small, specialist plant growers nowadays that wherever you go in the British Isles you are likely to come across one or other of them. The habits and characteristics of nurserymen were covered up to a point in Chapter 1, so it would be boring to churn it all out again here. Just remember, if you can, that because these special nurseries are so scattered and have such strange hours of business, it is unwise to plan a series of visits unless you give them plenty of notice. You must also expect them to be small and unimpressive-looking. One particularly good little nursery in, let's say for the sake of argument, Hawkhurst may well have a better collection of rare and beautiful plants than every garden centre in the whole of the south-east England. When you arrive there, all you can see are several empty frames in the foreground and a few little rows of pots and trays containing tiny embryonic plants. And yet, here you might find a Victorian primrose you thought lost to cultivation or a wild hybrid geranium multiplied by cuttings from a single plant discovered in the Biokov Mountains – just as thrilling – well nearly as thrilling – as finding the original and, after all, east Sussex is a lot more accessible than Dalmatia.

When it comes to legal acquisition from friends and acquaintances – as opposed to nicking – the secret is found in your tongue. 'Please may I have . . .' is how you start. Offering things in return is an excellent way of keeping material coming in. Very few gardens have nothing to offer and one of the finest ways of ensuring that all varieties stay in cultivation is to get them into as many gardens as possible. Anyone who is unwilling to spare any of their rare plant material to friends is not only a meanie twoshoes but a bad gardener into the bargain. There is no prestige in being the last person on earth to grow a vanishing variety, but just think of the glory of being named as the rescuer of one. A well-known example of this is the late Collingwood Ingram who rescued the magnificent Japanese cherry 'Tai Haku' from extinction. It has even been re-introduced to Japan.

The world of garden plant conservation is as richly peopled with cranks as the world of wildlife conservation. There are, luckily for the plants, some sensible, helpful and useful people who devote enormous amounts of time to ensuring that some of the most precious plant names don't forsake our gardens for the library shelf to be pored over by students in the future. The National Council for the Conservation of Plants and Gardens (NCCPG) is a self-appointed body of guardians of our floral heritage. Their work is of vital importance to all those who care about such things and is carried on with minimal funds and a great deal of personal effort. However, there are, as with all conserving organisations, problems. Some of the plant naming is chaotic. Frequently, names are ascribed to plants which match up to written descriptions in old reference books. If a plant is hard to match up to a colour photograph, you can imagine how much more difficult it is to match it to a couple of sentences written a hundred years ago – and then probably by a nineteenth-century TP who was well into his dotage.

Then there are the national collections. As you develop your expertise and begin to achieve recognition, people will begin to introduce themselves with the words 'I hold the National Collection of . . .'. Don't be scared off by this. It doesn't mean anything official but simply that they have been nominated by the NCCPG to accommodate a particular genus. Few national collections are very complete and with a number of plants – especially those that hybridise promiscuously like columbines or primulas – the idea of putting all the rare ones together in a small space is begging for trouble. The pitfall is that the rest of us, those who don't hold any 'national' collections, tend to relax, thinking the plants are safeguarded elsewhere. Don't you believe it. Every single gardener in Britain should regard himself as a conservator.

In this computer age, the concept of siting an individual collection of each genus is as archaic as having firemen on electric trains. The strength of the NCCPG is in its membership, not in its 'national collections'. A *truly* national catalogue of member gardens which house any one of a list of endangered plants is the way to do it. The list could be cross-referenced and updated every two years. Then, if one garden suffered a calamity, the chances of the whole collection of anything being damaged are minimal.

By now, your gardening expertise should be blossoming gloriously. You will be able to start building up your collection right away. Here are a few suggestions.

1 Select and prepare the equipment described earlier in the

chapter. Remember, golfing umbrellas hold more than any other – folding umbrellas are useless. Polythene is silent in the pocket – other plastic films rustle loudly, especially when there is a security man nearby.

2 Practise holding your cuttings knife with the blade pointing to the palm of your hand – rather like a factory worker trying to conceal a lighted cigarette – and learn to take cuttings with it in this position, with your back to the stock plant you are raiding. Once your skill is perfected, you should be able to bow to the Queen at a garden party and swipe a pelargonium cutting at the same time. While you are actually developing this skill, it is wise to carry a few bandaids with you.

3 Go to a good travel agent and collect as many brochures as you can. Ignore the ones for Sorrento and Majorca but pick up leaflets on Nepal, Sikkim, China and Tasmania. Be sure to leave these lying about the house in prominent positions. If you can leave a rucksack or two and some lederhosen lying about also, so much the better.

4 Go to a garden centre and buy as many packets of seeds as you can afford – avoid hybrids, just buy the species. Take the seeds out of the pretty packets and tip them into a selection of used manila envelopes. Add a pinch of dust and a few hayseeds to each for authenticity and label them with a blunt pencil, inventing location, date, altitude, etc. If you can fake a leopard footprint or two, this will help. This will ensure you have a good range of swaps. Just make sure the people with whom you swap haven't been up to the same trick. If their envelopes are labelled 'Shirley Poppies, collected Upper Ganges 1987, 20,000 feet' or something similar, be suspicious!

Chapter 9

Know your History

'Reminiscences can be boring, but . . .'

(Graham Stuart Thomas, *Perennial Garden Plants*, Dent,
1982 edition)

One of the many advantages of not having a degree in history is
that it enables you to be an open-minded historian. You're not
tied, hand and foot, to the demagoguery of ancient dons who
moulder away gracefully in our noble seats of learning. If you
happen to think that Henry VIII was a nice guy and a closet
women's libber, or that Thomas à Becket was a boring old fart,
well, fine. Nobody is going to ridicule you for that because you
have no status as a historian. But, start taking a few history courses
and the fetters are on. You have no choice but to go along with
whoever is inventing the history of the day.

These days, when gardening expertise means so much more
than simply being able to grow a straight parsnip, history of
horticulture plays a big role. An expert worth his salt should be
able to describe a plant in terms of its historical origins –
introduction date, where it was discovered, how it was acquired
and so forth. No doubt you have noticed the heavy output of
popular garden history that fills bookshop shelves these days,
much of it by writers whose training ended before O-level.

To most of us, history is a set of unrelated and inexplicable
phrases, sometimes linked to a date, often associated with
airless classrooms and comatose teachers. The Synod of Whitby,
Clarendon Code, Southsea Bubble, Star Chamber, Popish Plot or
Erasmus, for example, don't really mean much to one, although
I've a notion Erasmus might have invented shaving cream.
Naturally, we all remember the exciting or disgusting bits –
executing Catholics, executing Protestants, executing Thomas

More – just because he was a good guy, well, OK a bit of a monarch basher really – and, of course, the blowing up of the dissolute Lord Darnley, Mr Queen of Scots. But that's about it really, few of us even move beyond the stage where our teachers think it suitable to admit that Henry VIII died, not of over-eating but of syphilis.

All that is about to change, however. Read this chapter and you will emerge a truly erudite garden historian. Are you ready for the great draft of knowledge about to change your innermost being? Right, fine, now read on. By the way, provided you have been going though this book properly from front to back, this chapter will move you neatly to the end and you will have become a complete gardening expert. Isn't that the *most* exciting thing??? Now to the history . . .

Beginnings

Gardening is as old as mankind but nobody is quite sure how it all began. My favourite theory runs like this. About 50 or 60 thousand years ago, but possibly earlier – it could even have been before Mrs Thatcher became Prime Minister – a cave man was looking for a suitable bit of wood to use as a club. His old one was getting pretty clapped out and seemed to be spending more time at the club service station than in his hand these days. He was mooching around in a thicket somewhere between the Tigris and Euphrates when he tripped over a vine and bruised his toe. This enraged him to such an extent he tore it up by the roots and waved the strong trunk round his head until all the long traily bits had snapped off. He was left with a heavy piece of wood about the size and shape of a club.

'Ug,' he said, out loud, and then 'Errgh rrughh!' and took the wood home. It was a tidy walk from the Euphrates Valley to the home of the Cro-Magnon in the Dordogne but he completed the journey in the record time of sixteen years. On the way, he had time to do a bit of thinking. It occurred to him that if he had pulled this living vine out of the ground, it might grow again if he pushed it back in. When he got home he tried at once, digging a big hole and shoving the roots in. To his delight, the vine sprouted at once and, to his further delight, grew some wonderful bunches of grapes. He rushed into the cave to break the good news about the grapes to his wives and dog.

'Urgh Grerg seed forrg grow more clubs sprlrsh goarrhg licence to print money!' he burbled happily. What the caveman had meant was that this stumpy vine would produce lots of seeds which would also grow into splendid clubs. He was to become the first weapons magnate of pre-history.

Trouble was, the wretched wives kept eating the fruits before the seeds ripened. To prevent this, he pulled all the bunches off and shoved them into a large stone pot. But still the women were stealing the grapes so, in a fit of towering rage, he stamped on the fruit with his bare feet until it had become a pulpy mess. A month or two later, he collected the seeds, pouring the liquid into the dog's dish so that he could get at the seed-bearing pulp. The dog collapsed and died. The Caveman was so impressed with the toxicity of the juice, that he poured the rest of it into several small stone jars. What he couldn't know was that the dog, whose death had nothing to do with the juice, had suffered from a mild heart condition that suddenly worsened. He gave the jars to his enemies, pointing out that they were to use at parties. Stumped for a name, and presumably thinking of the dog at the time, he told the enemies the stuff was called whine. To his horror, the parties seemed to go with more pzazz than any had before and, as is usual with enemies, he wasn't invited. The new grape juice became all the rage and not the clubs.

Within the decade, everyone was growing vines from seed and the parties got wilder and wilder. The vine clubs got confused in people's minds with wine bars – later called crowbars – indeed, the club market went very flat until years later, when a neighbouring society of cavemen found out about the wine and came to raid. Threatened with superior clubs, the raiders settled for a trading partnership and swapped vines for apples and barley. Thus gardening, free trade and politics were born all at the same time.

From these beginnings horticulture developed smoothly. The effort of collecting nuts and berries from surrounding forests was too much of a fag, especially if you had a hangover, and people began to garden near their caves and, later, near their mud huts. Trees planted near settlements were guarded jealously and the first Tree Preservation Orders began to appear at about this time. As civilisation developed, the gardens got posher. However, it wasn't until the Ancient Egyptian Civilisation that garden expertise became a marketable commodity.

The Egyptian Queen Hatshepsut, apart from having an unpronounceable name, was a pretty nasty piece of work. When summoned to court, for example, you had to get her name right first time or it was instant death – if you were lucky. If she didn't like you, she'd get you started on a bit of stone carving on the inside of a tomb – *after* they'd sealed it up from the outside. But far worse for horticulture was her invention of containerised plants. She was the first to hit on the idea of keeping plants in pots, enabling them to be moved about. Hence, the beginnings of the garden centre trade – we have her to thank for that!

The Babylonians, also a nation devoted to capital punishment, hit on the idea of improving the amenity value of their public execution grounds. It would be more fitting, they felt, to make a series of beautiful gardens round the scaffolds. That way, families could enjoy picnicking and strolling in the gardens between events. These gardens became world famous and soon visitors from all around came to Babylon specially to see the Hanging Gardens whether there were any executions that day or not. Few days passed without several sentences being carried out, so an excellent amenity was backed up with a wealth of entertainment.

Thus, long before the Romans appeared in history, gardening had become a noble art. There were excellent private gardens where people grew fruit and veg as well as flowers, and also public pleasure gardens for everyone to enjoy – well, everyone except the slaves of course. They had no rights at all but had to work jolly hard to stay alive. On the other side of the world, China and Japan were busy gardening too, but we Westerners seemed unwilling to learn much about them until a few millenniums later. Of course, communications weren't quite so good in those days when the earth was flat and you could fall off the edge.

The Romans

It would be fair to say that today's gardening has its roots in Roman culture. A direct line runs from their gracious villas, through the Renaissance to modern classical design. It's a pity we hear so much about the nasty depraved Romans like Tiberius, Caligula and Nero and so little about the ones that helped to make the Roman Empire what it was before the decline. Well-to-do Romans certainly enjoyed lounging around on their patios. They also grew a great many herbs and medicinal plants.

Most of the information we have about Roman gardening comes from the pens of an uncle and nephew team known as Pliny. Well, not actually from their pens because they were too tired to carry them, but from the pens of their walking dictaphones. In those pre-Sanyo days you had a scribe, tablet at the ready, following you around wherever you went so that every gem of wisdom could be written into the wax as it fell from your lips. Pliny the Elder was quite a character. He abhorred time wasting and feverishly recorded every fragment of information he could find. This meant sending scouts all over the world to explore and come back to report. It was a well-known fact in Rome in those days, that if you didn't bring some pretty juicy information home you were likely to become a victim of the Roman Games which were grisly to say the least. Think of Twickenham when Wales is losing to the All Blacks and you are half-way to what it was like. To avoid such a dreadful fate, Pliny's messengers brought back ridiculous tales of myths and monsters which he set down as the Whole Truth in a mass of volumes which, for the next thousand years, was rated as the authoritative work on just about every aspect of natural history. Needless to say, much of the information was made up by the messengers to save their necks.

Roman villas had enclosed gardens with fountains and statues. They were quite fond of straight lines and had a large number of fruit trees incorporated into their planting plans. They were also quite big on poisons. Getting rid of people in power, when there are no elections, is quite an awkward business and, more often than not, a touch of poison can save a great deal of political strife. Augustus Caesar's wife, Livia, was a hot shot at poisoning and even decided to help her husband out of office and into Elysium. He was well up to her tricks and had a bevy of poor unfortunate food tasters round him for every meal. Eventually, he became so neurotic about her, he stopped eating proper meals altogether and lived in his orchard eating only fruit he picked himself. But even that didn't save him because the crafty old bag nobbled the fruit while it was still on the trees. Well, that's the theory according to Robert Graves and other scholars anyway. However, those of us who don't live in ivory towers would know that a diet of nothing but figs could bring down a man with the constitution of an ox and that further poisons would be quite unnecessary.

Many of our pretty garden plants were introduced into England by the Romans. We also have them to thank for some of our nastiest weeds including fat hen and nettles. Because they spread everywhere – the Romans I mean, not the weeds – their gardening fashion went with them too. They also picked up some pretty good ideas from other places like Persia, Carthage, Greece and Egypt. It looked as though the world was set for a good, steady progress into further civilisation. However, the Romans went into decline. Not being a proper historian, I can't tell you why and, anyway, you probably know far more about it than I do. Some historians have suggested that lead poisoning might be implicated. This is clearly fallacious because their chariots were not fuelled with leaded petrol. Anyway, whatever the cause, one minute they ruled the world, the next they were collapsing in an orgy of decadence that finished them off in 400 short years.

Then came the Dark Ages. Very dark, they were. For some reason, the sun never shone and everyone crept about in the mire. Civilisation was on the run, people began to indulge in Sunday trading and forgot to change their underwear. Eventually, they gave up underwear altogether and squatted, terrified, in rude hovels waiting for a despotic baron to steal their last crust or a Viking raid to commit acts of rape and pillage.

Gardening? Who had time for gardening? Everyone was too busy trying to be film extras for historic epics about Kirk Douglas and Charlton Heston. Gardening was dead and done for until the Renaissance. Don't ask me what people ate, because as well as growing things, the culinary arts were dead too. The Great MacDonald had not yet come down from the wild north to start mincing hedgehogs – that was not to happen until much later – and 'wimpy' was just another name for the rude hovels people called their homes. Happily, the light eventually dawned, the sun came out and the Vikings migrated back to Scandinavia to make lager commercials. The world of Art, Music, Literature and of course, Gardening, was about to enjoy another birth – if a birth is something to be enjoyed, that is.

The Renaissance

It all began in Italy. In Padua to be exact. Or was it Pisa. Yes, I think I lean towards Pisa. One morning, a cringing peasant was squatting in the mud waiting to see whether the camera crew for the third remake of *Ben Hur* might pass his way. After a couple of hours, it was getting a bit chilly so he decided to make up a little song to amuse himself. Here's how it went:

> Beautiful Sun with thy golden rays,
> To God, the wise Creator, be all praise;
> For thou nourisheth all the creation,
> Wherever there is to be found to be animation,
>
> Thou cheerest the weary traveller while on his way
> During the livelong summer day,
> As he admires the beautiful scenery while passing along,
> And singing to himself a stave of a song.

(Genuine extract from 'The Beautiful Sun' by William McGonagall)

A passerby heard this and said, 'That's a good little number you've got there. I'll build an organ so we can set it to music properly.'

'All right,' said the peasant. 'You get started on that and I'll go and see about taking out a copyright.'

Within a short time they had started a conservatoire of music and designed Venice. As it happened, they'd had a bit of a problem picking the right spot for Venice. The organ maker wanted to build on the north-west side of Italy but it seemed that site had been bagged by the world's first female city architect, Cherry Genoa.

'We'll have to make do with this spot,' he said, jabbing a pencil through a map of the marshes on the east side of the boot.

'Bit boggy, isn't it?'

'Sure, but think of the tourist potential. We can organise boat rides to all the best bits.'

This new wave of culture vulturing spread like wildfire and, within the century, most of Europe was into the Arts with a swing. Each of the quality newspapers printed an entire Arts page every day and fresh ideas were constantly bubbling up in new and fertile minds.

'Why don't we teach Arts and Sciences at the schools?'

'Can't.'

'Why on earth not?'

'We haven't got any schools.'

'Why don't we build some then?'

'Ah. Good point. Never thought of that.'

'Well, come on. Get a move on. There's a Renaissance on, you know.'

Meanwhile, things in England were still pretty uncivilised. We do know that Henry VI fostered education of a sort at this time. He founded a couple of rather snobbish little schools, and, in so doing, secured free tickets to Cambridge for his nobility who were otherwise too thick to pass the entrance exams. The tradition of breeding both national heroes and national traitors in roughly equal proportions at these places continues to this day.

However, when the Italians were beginning to reintroduce the rest of the world to civilisation, England was in the grip of the Wars of the Roses. These were based on family squabbles which began when the Plantagenet family fell out with each other over what colour of roses to plant in the dual carriageway central reservations. The north-eastern half wanted white rugosas but the Morecambe Bay lot insisted on *Rosa gallica*. This squabbling went on for decades until finally, after thousands of roses had been planted (red on the M6 and white on the A1), the then king, Richard III, recognised that there would be a serious shortage of rose fertiliser. In 1485 he headed south to Leicestershire, where a lot of horsebreeding went on, and arranged for a job lot to be dumped on a large field at Market Bosworth. His fair-weather friend, Lord Stanley, had been appointed to supervise the delivery but – and we shall never know whether this was deliberate or by genuine mistake – on the appointed day, he delivered the material to the Duke of Richmond, one Henry Tudor, by mistake. Richard was furious and charged about Market Bosworth doing frenzied Lawrence Olivier impersonations and, at one point, even offered his kingdom in exchange for a load of horse (manure). Richmond was quick to accept this offer and, after burying Richard alive in his rose fertiliser, gleefully accepted the kingdom. Thus, the Tudor Dynasty came to power.

After gaining the throne, in spite of being something of a misery guts, Henry got things going on the Renaissance front. Later,

when Henry VIII came to power, gardens were beginning to
blossom up and down the country. Hampton Court was a fine
example of sixteenth-century gardening and Sir Thomas More's
little cabbage patch at Chelsea even better. Indeed, many eminent
historians believe that More's imprisonment and subsequent
execution had nothing whatever to do with his refusal to go along
with the king's matrimonial plans, but was because his garden was
better than Henry's and Henry was just jealous. Elizabeth reigned
in a golden age of knot gardens. Gerard was beginning to
plagiarise his herbal from earlier works in these days and
Christopher Marlowe was writing Shakespeare's plays – or was it
the other way round?

The Tudors went out, the Stuarts came in. Politically, they were
a disaster. James I was said never to have washed his hands and to
have dribbled. Charles I lost his head over who was to govern –
him or Parliament. Charles II was merrie and fond of oranges –
especially Nell Gwyn's oranges. James II was not a bit merrie and
a religious bigot. The Glorious Revolution in 1688 brought in the
Oranges – no, not the Nell Gwyn oranges, the Dutch Oranges –
who were called William and Mary.

Despite the years of political unrest, the seventeenth century
was a good one for gardens. One of their main uses during the
Restoration was for canoodling. The gardens at Vauxhall were
especially well known for this and it was not advisable for any lone
females to be spotted there. The idea was to go in a group and not
to fan out until you each had a reliable partner. Pickpockets were
said to have done excessively well there because of the numbers of
pairs of unoccupied breeches hanging on the bushes.

Various big horticultural names emerged in the seventeenth
century, among them the Tradescants. They were father and son
and both keen plantsmen. Tradescant the Younger was one of the
first to go collecting in the new colonies at Virginia. While there,
he developed his instrumental skills and formed the first trad jazz
band which played one-night stands in small clubs. It is surprising
that this form of music was unknown by most people until
rediscovered and publicised in Louisiana nearly 200 years later.
Trad the Younger found many useful plants including columbines
and, wait for it, tradescantia. He also collected sea shells and other
oddments, thus starting the craze for bric à brac that has plagued
the English ever since.

From the later time of William and Mary to George IV, the English style of gardening was gaining ground. Before then, it had been all French – parterres, fountains and ooh la la! The French approach was to take a piece of beautiful countryside, build a chateau on it and then cut down every tree and bush within sight. Hills and hollows were levelled, after which new trees and hedges were planted in symmetrical rows. This unnatural layout was then embellished with huge, flat terraces crisscrossed and curlicued with fussy lines of low-growing shrublets and grass. It took about twenty gardeners per square metre to maintain these eyesores and if anyone went a bit wrong on the hedge cutting, the flaw in the pattern persisted for years. Louis XIV, during the odd moments he spent away from his mistresses, was obsessed with waterworks. At Maintenon he designed, and very nearly finished, a mammoth aqueduct to pipe water from there to Versailles some 20 miles away! He very nearly finished off the local workforce too.

The English approach, when it was adopted, was the very antithesis of all this. Parterres and knots were often swept away to make room for natural landscapes with lakes, bumps, hollows and grottoes. By the time the nineteenth century had begun, the English style was influencing world gardening. Thus, some of the best English gardens are in Sri Lanka, Australia and Jamaica. The basic design is rooted in the English love of plants. We tend to get the plants first and then wonder where on earth to plant them. The result of this random space-filling is delightful, especially where a vestige or two remains of the earlier formality, acting as a kind of restraint to the jungle within.

Just when we were settling down to a comfortably natural style, where gardens were places for pleasure and relaxation, blow me if the dreaded Victorian Era didn't rear its ugly and vociferous head. The last of the great Georgian gardeners was a frenzied Scot called John Claudius Loudon. Being a nature lover and an eminent plantsman, his designs had the effect of enhancing natural beauty rather than restricting it. He had poor health for much of his life and lost his right arm at the age of twenty-five. In spite of this he managed to work a sixteen-hour day and can be looked on as being the father of amateur gardening as we know it. He produced the first gardeners' magazine and created a huge encyclopedia – a sort of gardening *Mrs Beeton* – which was eagerly taken up by the newly developing middle classes.

But Loudon's influence was to be knocked neatly on the head for another 60 years. A particularly pushy, upwardly mobile young man was working for the Duke of Devonshire at Chatsworth. His name was Joseph Paxton and, like his striped-shirted counterparts of today, ostentation was his forte. He favoured planting eyeball-shrivelling masses of brilliant bedding plants – all jammed together to form a carpet. He was entirely self-taught, but extremely clever. He designed a good many Victorian edifices including the largest cucumber frame known to personkind – the Crystal Palace. He also produced gardening magazines which were more racy than Loudon's and therefore sold more copies. Paxton's ideas of planting to swank caught on with the age. Everybody wanted to show how rich they were and gardens became restless and pretentious places with shouts of colour surrounded by grotesque evergreens.

Victorian fussiness still lingers in many of our public parks and gardens, on traffic islands and in front of places like Buckingham Palace. However, in the 1880s a backlash was developing. An irascible Irishman had fallen out with his boss and stormed off in a tantrum to Dublin whence he was nudged towards England and a new career in Regent's Park. His name was William Robinson. He was a confirmed bachelor with a fiery Irish temper and a finely developed penchant for raising the hackles of his readers. He began to write extremely rude things about architects in gardens, about tawdry bedding displays and all things artificial. People like poor old Nathanial Lloyd, a highly respected horticulturist of the time, came in for some stick because he liked clipped yews. Lloyd's book *Garden Craftsmanship in Yew and Box* gets dubbed 'the poorest book that has so far disgraced the garden', by Robinson in his *The English Flower Garden*. He goes on with more invective for several paragraphs. Oddly enough, a few years before he wrote all this, he had a clipped yew hedge himself at Gravetye Manor. You can be sure he was careful to dig it up and move it before lunging his verbal stiletto at Lloyd, *Country Life* and anyone else who disagreed with him.

Robinson lived to be 97 which, since he was crippled and syphilitic, was a reasonably ripe age. He also made himself rather rich; he'd been poor when he crossed the Irish Sea in his twenties. By the time he died he owned a substantial estate at Gravetye near East Grinstead. He also had a half-track Citroën specially built so that he could whizz round the estate, driving over deadly banks and rough ground in order to frighten the daylights out of his passengers.

The other great figure of this period — far greater than almost anyone before or since, in fact – was a rather dumpy woman called Gertrude Jekyll. She is always reverently referred to in gardening literature as *Miss* Jekyll, and wherever she is discussed – and she still is, quite a lot – it is in hushed, respectful tones. Well you, my dear and most patient reader, may have noticed here and there a marginal lack of respect in this book. I'm afraid Miss Humpty Bumpty is long overdue for a bit of leg pull as well. But don't get me wrong, she was a great gardener and had an enormous influence. Indeed, most of us still garden in, more or less, the Jekyll manner. That's the problem. In her day one could get flocks of skilled gardeners who worked away for a penny a fortnight. Her gardening is therefore very labour-intensive. For contemporaries of her social class, a hard day in the garden meant sitting on a bench with the head gardener saying, 'I'll have red tulips this spring and you can plant forget-me-nots between them like last year.'

'Yes Ma'am.'

'You will have to get Dick and Ned to mulch it all over with manure from the stables and I'm relying on you to select the bulbs.'

'Yes Ma'am.'

'Then there's the new shrubbery. Have you got the order made out?'

'Yes, Ma'am. It's all here ready for you to sign. And if you could make out and sign the cheque.'

'Oh, I'm not sure whether I've got enough strength left to do that today. All this gardening is *so* exhausting. Perhaps this afternoon, after my rest.'

'Very good, Ma'am.'

Old Ma Jekyll lived to a ripe age and was a close associate of Robinson's. She was an accomplished artist who had hobnobbed with people like William Morris – inventor of the half-timbered motor car – and Hector Brabazon, who designed and built the early Jumbo aircraft named after him. With these Pre-Raphaelite friends, it is not surprising that she soon took up silversmithery, needlework and ocean cruising. Alas, just when her career as an interior decorator was budding – she'd already done a job for the Grosvenors at Eaton Hall and for the gals at Girton College, Cambridge, and was hoping for a nice little contract like one of the new Barratt estates in Berkshire, when disaster struck. Her eyesight was failing and, after sound advice from an eminent eye specialist in Wiesbaden, she had to give up painting and all other forms of close work. However, now that she could no longer paint, she read and wrote copiously! She also took to designing gardens. One wonders whether any of today's eminent garden designers might not perform a little better if they were visually handicapped.

Just as her career in garden design was progressing really well, she suffered another disastrous blow. The architect Edwin Lutyens came into her life. Lutyens was soon to move abroad to design a new deli for General Foods who were keen to get into upmarket cooked foods. Meanwhile, so taken with William Morris's half-timbered small family car, he set about building as many early-twentieth-century half-timbered houses as he could. (Building castles was to come later, after the chain of delis.) One day, when he was just checking up on a mock-Tudor residence near Godalming, he noticed Miss Bumps, as she was called, emerging backwards from under an elder bush.

'Good God!' he cried. 'The very person I'm looking for. Come and plant up these gardens I've designed.'

'Shan't!' said Miss J. But before long she had fallen under his spell and was trying desperately to fit a shrub or two into his extraordinarily complicated mishmashes of stone ballustrading, paths, terraces, flagstones and narrow gutters. These latter devices, called rills, were too narrow to plan properly or to house fish but were really meant to lead your eye from whatever place you were standing to the house so that you could admire the great architect's masterpiece. The Lutyens–Jekyll partnership was to run for years during which about a hundred gardens were designed jointly. As so often happens with famous artists, many more gardens claim to be Jekyll–Lutyens gardens than really are.

Leaving aside Lutyens and the garden edifices, Gertrude Jekyll's genius lay in her accurate judgement of which plants would look right together. Her colour sense was unerring and she was quite dotty about plants of all kinds – not just the smart garden varieties but wild species too. She appraised them for their scent and foliage quality as well as for their flowers. When she died, in

1932, the age of prosperous gardening was drawing to a close. There were sinister noises coming out of Germany, the great depression was deepening and unemployment soaring.

A huge contribution to horticulture was made, during the nineteenth and early twentieth centuries, by the great plant hunters. These brave men, many of them from very well-cushioned backgrounds, risked and sometimes lost their lives finding new species for our gardens. We've already glanced at the Tradescant boys but most of the famous collectors lived much later. Most were after plants that would thrive in our rotten climate, which meant mountain climbing or visiting latitudes where a cold damp season lasted for ten months of the year.

Joseph Banks was an early collector, living nearly a century before the spate of hunting went on in China. As the name suggests, he was indescribably rich and everyone thought he would spend his life sitting about being waited on hand and foot by lackeys. Not a bit of it. As soon as he left Oxford he was off to foreign parts. He took the 'dismal climate' quest a bit far, making his first expedition to Labrador where he enjoyed all sorts of adventures including getting lost in the snow and being found by the famous Labrador retrievers. He collected all sorts of plants in Labrador and Newfoundland and, partly for that reason but mainly because he was extremely well off, was elected to the Royal Society. It was a bit easier to get in in those days than it is today!

Once he'd got back from North America, the wanderlust was embedded in his soul so, without further ado, he planned another trip, this time even more dangerous and daring, to Wales, where he collected the first dresser to be seen in polite English society. The next excursion was a little longer and landed him in Australia with Captain Cook. While they were there they dined on kangaroo and founded Surfers' paradise. He was amazed to find plants there called *banksias*. Wasn't that a coincidence?

About a hundred years later, some Jesuit missionaries found themselves in a remote and dangerous spot in China. As well as saving the souls of lots of heathen Chinese, they had time to study the local flora. The most famous of these was Père David. He was a fanatical naturalist and that's why a host of things are named after him: Père David's deer, *Buddleia davidii,* and *Davidia involucrata.*

Jean Marie Delavay was also a missionary who spent more time plant hunting than peddling Catholicism. He spent most of his life in Yunnan where he found plenty to keep him amused. He caught bubonic plague, lost an arm and suffered countless other hardships, only to see much of his precious seed material killed through mismanagement by the authorities at the Paris Jardin des Plantes. This could be one reason why it was turned into a zoo – they thought they'd have better luck with animals than with plants.

Paul Guillaume Farges collected a staggering 4,000 species in a single decade, and poor old Jean André Soulié went collecting a bit too near the Sino-Tibetan border where the Tibetan monks took exception to his religion and tortured and shot him.

Slightly later, at the turn of the century, the famous Ernest Henry 'Chinese' Wilson began his eventful plant-hunting expeditions. His luck was not especially good. In 1899, he set off to find the famous pocket handkerchief tree described by David. He got directions from another collector called Henry the Navigator (I've never been able to find out what his surname was) and set off over inhospitable territory. Soon he was arrested and locked up for spying. He managed to prove his innocence, but after that experience was careful to avoid the local natives like the plague. However, the plague was just what he didn't avoid – most of his party died of fever. He took a boat but found out too late that the boatman was an opium addict who, during a drug-induced trance, crashed the boat onto rocks in the rapids. Finally, after all these disasters, Wilson arrived at the spot where the *Davidia involucrata* tree was supposed to have been. All he found was a stump because the natives had recently chopped it down to use as building material for one of their houses. This gave Wilson a feeling of mild frustration but his reward was soon to follow because elsewhere, at Ichang to be exact, he found lots of handkerchief trees growing where he least expected them, a short walk from where he was living. This discovery helped to take his mind off the savage Boxer Rebellion that was happening all round him.

If you think Wilson had a rough time, you should see what happened to George Forrest. He went hunting near the Tibetan border at a time when the Tibetans were murdering every Chinese they could get their hands on, and they considered Europeans to be even less desirable! Of his team of seventeen, he was the only survivor and had to run away into the forest, pursued for days by bloodthirsty bandits aided by tracker dogs. With that mob behind him it is hardly surprising that though he pierced his foot right through with a bamboo spike, he didn't even stop. What was doubly disappointing was the fact that most of his plants were too tender to survive the British climate.

It was during these big collecting years that Rhodomania caught hold of half the gardening population. Rhododendrons, a lifelong obsession with far too many gardeners, began to smother the banks and glades of otherwise attractive gardens. Every day, a new species or hybrid was introduced, usually from China. Luckily, many of us garden on limy soil and are able to escape them but there was a time when the leafier suburbs of London were in danger of disappearing under a neo-Himalayan under-storey of gargantuan proportions. Every June, the most garish colours would scream from every corner – flesh tones, purples, scarlets, whites, yellows and unimaginable bi-colours with speckles, streaks and blobs of colour in their throats. Then, for the remaining eleven months the same suburbs would subside to a sombre, suicidal bottle-green. Nothing looked right growing with these dreary bushes, little grew under their dense shade and even their nectar proved to be poisonous to our English honey bees. Rhodomania lives on to this day, but now the race is on to breed the smallest races from the *yakushimanum* hybrids – nicknamed the 'yaks' – an ugly name, even for rhododendrons.

One of the most appealing aspects of Reginald Farrer, another great collector, was that he did not introduce any rhododendrons – or not many anyway. He had as harrowing a time as the rest of them, after a very comfortable and privileged background, and met a tragic and premature end. When he was twenty-seven he went to Ceylon and got religion. He became a Buddhist, much to the annoyance of his parents who were devout Protestants. He teamed up with another collector from Kew called William Purdom and they too went to dice with death, dodging the natives on the Tibetan border. Purdom even disguised himself as a coolie so that he could nip into Tibet without getting scragged or pinch some seed from the 'flannel' buddleia which grew over the border. It seems unfair that it was then called *Buddleia farreri* and not *B. purdomiana.*

Farrer wanted to do a lot more hunting in Yunnan later, but

George Forrest was hunting there and forbade anyone else to invade his territory. After all, it belonged to Forrest, didn't it? The Chinese? What on earth did it have to do with them? As second choice, he went to the mountains in Burma where the weather was humid and cold. He caught a fatal bout of pneumonia in a place called Nyitadi and that was the end of him.

There were so many more plant hunters but not enough room here to tell you about them all. Most had adventurous times and many met unexpectedly violent ends. The results of their work are to be seen in the rich variety of plants in our gardens.

The modern age of horticulture was heralded by such great names as Vita Sackville-West, Edward 'Gussie' Bowles and Adam the Gardener. Vita Sackville-West was a complete amateur who learnt the job as she went along. That didn't prevent her from making, with her husband Harold Nicolson, one of the finest gardens in the world at Sissinghurst. When they bought the farm there, most of the living accommodation was in ruins and the garden simply didn't exist. However, Vita soon got busy with her plants while Harold laid out the formal bits. The interesting thing about Sissinghurst is that the planting is not only highly labour intensive, it also consists of a series of courtyards and enclosures that are inaccessible to trolleys or wheelbarrows. Everything has to be carried about in boxes and baskets, or winched out by helicopter. Vita and Harold pioneered opening to the public. In those pre-war days they called the visitors 'shillingses'. Nowadays they are called 'threepoundses'.

Little is known about the private life of Edward Augustus 'Gussie' Bowles. He was certainly a confirmed bachelor and was born and lived and died in the same house in the heart of rural Middlesex. He was a bit of an asthmatic, so going off plant collecting in the mountains was good for his physical health as well as his mental well being. Work? No, as you've probably noticed, few of these eminent horticulturists actually had to work for a living. They just tinkered about happily in their gardens while a useful private income sustained them. Bowles was a crocus man. He was also good on snowdrops, cochicums and daffodils. By the time he was 36 he had 135 species of crocus in coldframes in his garden. He was a TP *par excellence,* giving full support to the Royal Horticultural Society and becoming a member of their

scientific committee. The fact that he had no scientific qualifications at all – not even O-level biology – suggests that he either
taught himself pretty thoroughly or else throws some doubt on the
validity of the RHS scientific committee of the day.

Adam the Gardener was a newspaper strip character. Of course
you remember him. You'll be lying about your age next!

Well, according to leading horticulturists of today, good gardening
more or less stopped with E. A. Bowles. Not true, of course. You
might just as well say that art ended with Cézanne or music with
Debussy. There are plenty of good modern gardeners but most of
them maintain properties which were built along the lines of great
gardens of the past. The next move will be someone to invent a
form of gardening that matches up to today's quality and
availability of labour. Clearly, the interest in plants is still growing
vigorously and the demand for new introductions, improved
varieties and unusual plants is brisker than ever before. All we
need now is for some eminent plantsman to say, 'Never mind a few
weeds – they are acceptable these days as long as the plants can
flourish in reasonably natural surroundings.'

Several eminent garden experts also dislike park-like displays of
bedding plants. But park-like displays can look quite good in parks
if not in front gardens. The problem is usually not that bedding
plants are used each year but that such unimaginative planting
schemes are adhered to. There is no excuse for this – the choice of
tender plants suitable for annual planting has never been richer.
I wonder what Shakespeare would make of the corporation
bedding schemes at Stratford today. Imagine a modern *Midsummer
Night's Dream:*

> I know a bank where the carpet bedding grows,
> Where red and yellow annuals clash in rows,
> Quite ruined at its edge with blue and white,
> For clumps of Alyssum must slog it out
> With royal-blue Lobelia rank on rank.
> There lies Titania, eyelids screwed up tight,
> Trying to blot out this awful sight!

This is rather an emotionally charged moment, isn't it? Here we
are, about to part company. You to launch yourself as a fully
fledged gardening expert, me to go off and study English grammar

at our village primary school before teaching a coarse (sic) in garden history. If you have read every word of the foregoing with care and attention, you should have no trouble convincing all you meet that you are, in truth, a well-grounded expert. I should carry this book around in your pocket for a few months if I were you, just until your ego has grown enough for you to survive without props or crutches. Happy Gardening!

At Chelsea, you get to glimpse the royals.